Is There Life
Before Death?

(I was An Imaginary Playmate in My Past Lives)

Compiled by

Steve Andreas

Real People Press

Front cover photo and illustrations by Steve Andreas.
Back cover photo by Moses Street.

ISBN: 0-911226-34-6 clothbound $19.95

Library of Congress Cataloging-in-Publication Data:

Is there life before death? : (I was an imaginary playmate in my past lives) / compiled by Steve Andreas.
    p. cm.
    Includes index.
    ISBN 0-911226-34-6
    1. Conduct of life. 2. Self-actualization (Psychology)
I. Andreas, Steve.
BG637.C5I8   1995
158'.1—dc20   95-15312
                                              CIP

This book is dedicated to all of us,
on this difficult journey
for which we are so poorly prepared.
We need all the help we can get.

Contents

Choose life—
Only that
And always
And at whatever risk.

To let life leak out
To let it wear away
By the mere passage of time
To withhold giving it and spreading it
Is to choose nothing.

—Sister Mary Corita Kent

Introduction

In the cliff dwellings of the desert southwest, the red sandstone walls and ceilings often bear muddy handprints, mute testimony to the people who labored there thousands of years ago. Protected from wind and rain—the messengers of time—each detail is as clear as if the hands had placed them yesterday. Why did someone pause from bonding stone with mud to leave these prints?

In the white limestone caves of Lascaux, in France, are outlines of hands made by spraying pigment through a straw while a hand was held flat against the wall. These hands paused not from building walls, but from creating marvelous images of the large animals that sustained their lives—horses, deer, and bison. Working by torchlight, deep underground, why did these hands pause to leave images of themselves, some 30,000 years ago? Although we can only guess, perhaps those handprints are saying quietly, "I was here; I lived."

The handprints in this book are made with words, rather than mud or pigment. Before I move on, I want to leave behind some bits of what I have learned, and to preserve the words of others that have moved me and sustained me on my journey—in the hope that those who come after might find some of them useful. Buckminster Fuller said it well:

"What do I know about what I am, what each of us is?" And I went back very quickly to the realization of humanity being born naked, helpless, ignorant—being hungry and thirsty and curious, to drive us to learn by trial and error. We have to make an enormous number of mistakes to get anywhere. We haven't any idea how long it took to get words, so that we could help each other with information that we had been learning from our mistakes. It was only about 8,000 years ago that writing was invented so that those who were dead could tell the living what they had found out."[1]

I chose the title for this book over twenty years ago, and I have been collecting favorite stories, quotes, and poems for at least twice that span. One of the nicest compliments I've received was when a friend of mine said, "I think of you as my bloodhound; the things you sniff out have usually been things I want to know about." When I have not found others' words to speak for me, I have done my best to set down my own thoughts. The words in this book are those that have touched me, opened me to beauty, or reminded me of truths forgotten. As Barry Lopez writes, in *Crow and Weasel:*

"The stories people tell have a way of taking care of them. If stories come to you, care for them. And learn to give them away where they are needed. Sometimes a person needs a story more than food to stay alive. That is why we put these stories in each other's memory. This is how people

[1]"A Week with Buckminster Fuller" audiotape set. Kirkwood Meadows, August 17-22, 1981, © 1981 Buckminster Fuller.

2

care for themselves. One day you will be good storytellers. Never forget these obligations."[2]

Although there is a sequence to the pieces in this book, they can be read in any order. Of course some will appeal to you and some not, and you will surely recognize some you have read before. These are the words that I have found I can read over and over again, over many years, with deepening appreciation. When you find one that moves you, pause to savor it before moving on.

It would be easy to assume that because a writer has found wise words, that s/he also has a wise life. More often it is the reverse; the words are born out of a recognition of what is possible, but not yet attained, and set down as reminders of what is worthwhile to continue to work toward. Rainer Maria Rilke said it well in *Letters to a Young Poet:*

"Do not believe that he who seeks to comfort you lives untroubled among the simple and quiet words that sometimes do you good. His life has much difficulty and sadness and remains far behind yours. Were it otherwise he would never have been able to find those words."[3]

Some of you may notice that the design and layout of this book bears some similarity to that of Hugh Prather's first book *Notes to Myself,* which I designed twenty-five years ago. Similar designs were also used in several of his later books.

[2]Excerpt from CROW AND WEASEL, by Barry Lopez and illustrated by Tom Pohrt. Text copyright © 1990 by Barry Lopez. Reprinted by permission of North Point Press, a division of Farrar, Straus & Giroux, Inc.
[3]Reprinted from LETTERS TO A YOUNG POET by Rainer Maria Rilke, translated from the German by M. D. Herter Norton, with the permission of W. W. Norton & Co., Inc. Copyright 1934 by W. W. Norton & Company, Inc., renewed 1962 by M. D. Herter Norton. Revised edition copyright 1954 by W. W. Norton & Company, Inc.

I have done my best to track down the authors and sources of all the pieces in this book, but some are still noted "author unknown" (AU) or "source unknown" (SU), and a few selections may even be misidentified. If you know the author or source of any such piece, please write to me in care of the publisher, so that I can give proper credit in future printings.

Finally, if something in this book has moved or touched you, and you know of some story, quote or poem that you think I might enjoy, please send it to me in care of the publisher. I'm sure there must be many more wonderful pieces that haven't yet washed up on the shore of my living.

—Steve Andreas

4

Embezzle The Sun

"... and follow the meanders of the stream ..."
Oh, phrase of freshness, brief poetic glint
Contained in a dry legal instrument
Where contrast makes its simple beauty gleam
On old surveys whose designations seem
To fix the boundaries of lost content,
What moving hand by happy accident
Responded to a mind that paused to dream?

I like to think the weary clerk who wrote
The April words that dusty records show
Embezzled the sun of many a morning beam
And spent them on a little fishing boat
And made good his escape in time to go
"And follow the meanders of the stream."

—Robert Lee Brothers

From *Robert Lee Brothers: The Collected Poems* edited by Susan Ford Wiltshire, Ph.D. (in preparation).

A Path With a Heart

A path is only a path; if you feel you should not follow it, you must not stay with it under any conditions. To
have such clarity you must lead a disciplined life. Only
then will you know that any path is only a path, and there
is no affront, to oneself or to others, in dropping it if that is
what your heart tells you to do. But your decision to keep
on the path or to leave it must be free of fear or ambition.
I warn you. Look at every path closely and deliberately.
Try it as many times as you think necessary. This question
is one that only a very old man asks. My benefactor told
me about it once when I was young, and my blood was
too vigorous for me to understand it. Now I do understand
it. I will tell you what it is: Does this path have a heart?

All paths are the same: they lead nowhere. They are
paths going through the bush, or into the bush. In my
own life I could say I have traversed long, long paths, but
I am not anywhere. My benefactor's question has meaning now. Does this path have a heart? If it does, the path
is good; if it doesn't, it is of no use. Both paths lead

nowhere; but one has a heart, the other doesn't. One makes for a joyful journey; as long as you follow it, you are one with it. The other will make you curse your life. One makes you strong; the other weakens you. . . .

A path without a heart is never enjoyable. You have to work hard even to take it. On the other hand, a path with heart is easy; it does not make you work at liking it. . . . Before you embark on it you ask the question: Does this path have a heart? If the answer is no, you will know it, and then you must choose another path. . . . The trouble is nobody asks the question; and when a man finally realizes that he has taken a path without a heart, the path is ready to kill him. At that point very few men can stop to deliberate, and leave the path. . . .

For me there is only the traveling on paths that have heart, on any path that may have heart. There I travel, and the only worthwhile challenge is to traverse its full length. And there I travel, looking, looking, breathlessly.

—Carlos Casteneda

Are There Any Questions?

"Are there any questions?" An offer that comes at the end of college lectures and long meetings. Said when an audience is not only overdosed with information, but when there is no time left anyhow. At times like that you sure do have questions. Like, "Can we leave now?" and "What the hell was this meeting for?" and "Where can I get a drink?"

The gesture is supposed to indicate openness on the part of the speaker, I suppose, but if in fact you do ask a question, both the speaker and the audience will give you drop-dead looks. And some fool—some earnest idiot—always asks. And the speaker always answers. By repeating most of what he has already said.

But if there is a little time left and there is a little silence in response to the invitation, I usually ask the most important question of all: "What is the Meaning of Life?"

You never know, somebody may have the answer, and I'd really hate to miss it because I was too socially inhibited to ask. But when I ask, it's usually taken as a kind of absurdist move—people laugh and nod and gather up their stuff and the meeting is dismissed on that ridiculous note.

Once, and only once, I asked that question and got a serious answer. One that is with me still.

First, I must tell you where this happened, because the place has a power of its own. In Greece again.

Near the village of Gonia, on a rocky bay of the island of Crete, sits a Greek Orthodox monastery. Alongside it, on land donated by the monastery, is an institute dedicated to human understanding and peace, and especially to rapprochement between Germans and Cretans. An improbable task, given the bitter residue of wartime.

This site is important, because it overlooks the small airstrip at Maléme where Nazi paratroopers invaded Crete and were attacked by peasants wielding kitchen knives and hay scythes. The retribution was terrible. The populations of whole villages were lined up and shot for assaulting Hitler's finest troops. High above the institute is a cemetery with a single cross marking the mass grave of Cretan partisans. And across the bay on yet another hill is the regimented burial ground of the Nazi paratroopers. The memorials are so placed that all might see and never forget. Hate was the only weapon the Cretans had at the end, and it was a weapon many vowed never to give up. Never ever.

Against this heavy curtain of history, in this place where the stone of hatred is hard and thick, the existence of an institute devoted to healing the wounds of war is a fragile paradox. How has it come to be here? The answer is a man. Alexander Papaderos.

A doctor of philosophy, teacher, politician, resident of Athens but a son of this soil. At war's end he came to believe that the Germans and the Cretans had much to give one another—much to learn from one another. That they had an example to set. For if they could forgive each other and construct a creative relationship, then any people could.

To make a lovely story short, Papaderos succeeded. The institute became a reality—a conference ground on the site of horror—and it was in fact a source of productive interaction between the two countries. Books have been written on the dreams that were realized by what people gave to people in this place.

By the time I came to the institute for a summer session, Alexander Papaderos had become a living legend. One look at him and you saw his strength and intensity—energy, physical power, courage, intelligence, passion, and vivacity radiated from his person. And to speak to him, to shake his hand, to be in a room with him when he spoke, was to experience his extraordinary electric humanity. Few men live up to their reputations when you get close. Alexander Papaderos was an exception.

At the last session on the last morning of a two-week seminar on Greek culture, led by intellectuals and experts in their fields who were recruited by Papaderos from across Greece, Papaderos rose from his chair at the back of the room and walked to the front, where he stood in the bright Greek sunlight of an open window and looked out. We followed his gaze across the bay to the iron cross marking the German cemetery.

He turned. And made the ritual gesture: "Are there any questions?"

Quiet quilted the room. These two weeks had generated enough questions for a lifetime, but for now there was only silence.

"No questions?" Papaderos swept the room with his eyes.

So. I asked.

"Dr. Papaderos, what is the meaning of life?"

The usual laughter followed, and people stirred to go.

Papaderos held up his hand and stilled the room and looked at me for a long time, asking with his eyes if I was serious and seeing from my eyes that I was.

"I will answer your question."

Taking his wallet out of his hip pocket, he fished into a leather billfold and brought out a very small round mirror, about the size of a quarter.

And what he said went like this:

"When I was a small child, during the war, we were very poor and we lived in a remote village. One day, on the road, I found the broken pieces of a mirror. A German motorcycle had been wrecked in that place.

"I tried to find all the pieces and put them together, but it was not possible, so I kept only the largest piece. This one. And by scratching it on a stone I made it round. I began to play with it as a toy and became fascinated by the fact that I could reflect light into dark places where the sun would never shine—in deep holes and crevices and dark closets. It became a game for me to get light into the most inaccessible places I could find.

"I kept the little mirror, and as I went about my growing up, I would take it out in idle moments and continue the challenge of the game. As I became a man, I grew to understand that this was not just a child's game but a metaphor for what I might do with my life. I came to understand that I am not the light or the source of light. But light—truth, understanding, knowledge—is there, and it will only shine in many dark places if I reflect it.

"I am a fragment of a mirror whose whole design and shape I do not know. Nevertheless, with what I have I can reflect light into the dark places of this world—into the black places in the hearts of men—and change some things in some people. Perhaps others may see and do likewise. This is what I am about. This is the meaning of my life."

And then he took his small mirror and, holding it carefully, caught the bright rays of daylight streaming through the window and reflected them onto my face and onto my hands folded on the desk.

Much of what I experienced in the way of information about Greek culture and history that summer is gone from memory. But in the wallet of my mind I carry a small round mirror still.

Are there any questions?

—Robert Fulghum

Outwitted

He drew a circle that shut me out—
Heretic, rebel, a thing to flout.
But Love and I had the wit to win:
We drew a circle that took him in!

—Edwin Markham

From POEMS OF EDWIN MARKHAM, SELECTED AND ARRANGED by
CHARLES L. WALLIS. Copyright 1950 by Virgil Markham. Copyright renewed.
Reprinted by permission of HarperCollins Publishers, Inc.

Napoleon and the Furrier

During Napoleon's invasion of Russia, his troops were battling in the middle of yet another small town in that endless wintry land, when he was accidentally separated from his men. A group of Russian Cossacks spotted him, and began chasing him through the twisting streets. Napoleon ran for his life, and ducked into a little furrier's shop on a side alley. As Napoleon entered the shop, gasping for breath, he saw the furrier and cried piteously, "Save me, save me! Where can I hide?" The furrier said "Quick, under this big pile of furs in the corner," and covered Napoleon up with many furs.

No sooner had he finished when the Russian Cossacks burst in the door, shouting "Where is he? We saw him come in." Despite the furrier's protests, they tore his shop apart trying to find Napoleon. They poked into the pile of furs with their swords, but didn't find him. Soon they gave up and left.

After some time, Napoleon crept out from under the furs, unharmed, just as Napoleon's personal guards came in the door. The furrier turned to Napoleon and said timidly, "Excuse me for asking this question of such a great man, but what was it like to be under those furs, knowing that the next moment would surely be your last?" Napoleon drew himself up to his full height, and said to the furrier indignantly, "How could you ask such a question of me, the emperor Napoleon!! Guards, take this impudent man out, blindfold him, and execute him. I, myself, will personally give the command to fire!"

The guards grabbed the poor furrier, dragged him outside, stood him up against a wall, and blindfolded him. The furrier could see nothing, but he could hear the movements of the guards as they slowly shuffled into a line and prepared their rifles. He could hear the soft ruffling sound of his clothing in the cold wind, and he felt it tugging gently at his clothes and chilling his cheeks, and the uncontrollable trembling in his legs. Then he heard Napoleon clear his throat and call out slowly, "Ready, . . . aim. . . ." In that moment, knowing that even these few sensations were about to be taken from him forever, a feeling that he couldn't describe welled up in him, and tears poured down his cheeks.

After a long period of silence, the furrier heard footsteps approaching him, and the blindfold was stripped from his eyes. Still partially blinded by the sudden sunlight, he saw Napoleon's eyes looking deeply and intently into his own—eyes that seemed to see into every dusty corner of his being. Then Napoleon said softly, "Now you know."

—Steve and Connirae Andreas
(with thanks to Greg Brodsky)

15

The Listener
by John Berry

Once there was a puny little Czech concert violinist
named Rudolf, who lived in Sweden. Some of his friends
thought he was not the best of musicians because he was
restless; others thought he was restless because he was not
the best of musicians. At any rate, he hit upon a way of
making a living, with no competitors. Whether by choice
or necessity, he used to sail about Scandinavia in his small
boat, all alone, giving concerts in little seaport towns. If
he found accompanists, well and good; if not, he played
works for unaccompanied violin; and it happened once or
twice that he wanted a piano so badly that he imagined
one, and then he played whole sonatas for violin and
piano, with no piano in sight.

One year Rudolf sailed all the way out to Iceland and
began working his way around that rocky coast from one
town to another. It was a hard, stubborn land; but people
in those difficult places do not forget the law of hospital-
ity to the stranger—for their God may decree that they too
shall become strangers on the face of the earth. The audi-

Reprinted by permission of the author. First published in New World Writing
#16 (1960).

16

ences were small, and even if Rudolf had been really first-rate, they would not have been very demonstrative. From ancient times their energy had gone, first of all, into earnest toil. Sometimes they were collected by the local schoolteacher, who reminded them of their duty to the names of Beethoven and Bach and Mozart and one or two others whose music perhaps was not much heard in those parts. Too often people sat stolidly watching the noisy little fiddler, and went home feeling gravely edified. But they paid.

As Rudolf was sailing from one town to the next along a sparsely settled shore, the northeast turned black and menacing. A storm was bearing down upon Iceland. Rudolf was rounding a bleak, dangerous cape, and his map told him that the nearest harbor was half a day's journey away. He was starting to worry when he saw, less than a mile off shore, a lighthouse on a tiny rock island. At the base of the lighthouse was a deep narrow cove, protected by cliffs. With some difficulty, in the rising seas, he put in there and moored to an iron ring that hung from the cliff. A flight of stairs, hewn out of the rock, led up to the lighthouse. On top of the cliff, outlined against the scudding clouds, stood a man.

"You are welcome!" the voice boomed over the sound of the waves that were already beginning to break over the island.

Darkness fell quickly. The lighthouse keeper led his guest up the spiral stairs to the living room on the third floor, then busied himself in preparation for the storm. Above all, he had to attend to the great lamp in the tower, that dominated the whole region. It was a continuous light, intensified by reflectors, and eclipsed by shutters at regular intervals. The duration of light was equal to that of darkness.

The lighthouse keeper was a huge old man with a grizzled beard that came down over his chest. Slow, deliberate, bearlike, he moved without wasted motion about the limited world of which he was the master. He spoke little, as if words had not much importance compared to the other forces that comprised his life. Yet he was equable, as those elements were not.

After the supper of black bread and boiled potatoes, herring, cheese and hot tea, which they took in the kitchen above the living room, the two men sat and contemplated each other's presence. Above them was the maintenance room, and above that the great lamp spoke majestic, silent messages of light to the ships at sea. The storm hammered like a battering ram on the walls of the lighthouse. Rudolf offered tobacco, feeling suddenly immature as he did so. The old man smiled a little as he declined it by a slight movement of the head; it was as if he knew well the uses of tobacco and the need for offering it, and affirmed it all, yet—here he, too, was halfway apologetic—was self-contained and without need of anything that was not already within his power or to which he did not relinquish his power. And he sat there, gentle and reflective, his great workman hands resting on outspread thighs.

It seemed to Rudolf that the lighthouse keeper was entirely aware of all the sounds of the storm and of its violent impact upon the lighthouse, but he knew them so well that he did not have to think about them; they were like the involuntary movements of his own heart and blood. In the same way, beneath the simple courtesy that made him speak and listen to his guest in specific ways, he was already calmly and mysteriously a part of him, as surely as the mainland was connected with the little island, and all the islands with one another, so commodiously, under the ocean.

18

Gradually Rudolf drew forth the sparse data of the old man's life: He had been born in this very lighthouse eighty-three years before, when his father was the lighthouse keeper. His mother—the only woman he had ever known—had taught him to read the Bible, and he read it daily. He had no other books.

As a musician, Rudolf had not had time to read much either—but then, he had lived in cities. He reached down and took his beloved violin out of its case.

"What do you make with that, sir?" the old man asked.

For a second Rudolf thought his host might be joking; but the serenity of the other's expression reassured him. There was not even curiosity about the instrument, but rather a whole interest in him, the person, that included his "work." In most circumstances Rudolf would have found it hard to believe that there could exist someone who did not know what a violin was; yet now he had no inclination to laugh. He felt small and inadequate.

"I make—music with it," he stammered in a low voice.

"Music," the old man said ponderously. "I have heard of it. But I have never seen music."

"One does not see music. One hears it."

"Ah, yes," the lighthouse keeper consented, as it were with humility. This too was in the nature of things wherein all works were wonders, and all things were known eternally and were poignant in their transiency. His wide gray eyes rested upon the little fiddler and conferred upon him all the importance of which any individual is capable.

Then something in the storm and the lighthouse and the old man exalted Rudolf, filled him with compassion, and love and a spaciousness infinitely beyond himself. He

19

wanted to strike a work of fire and stars into being for the old man. And, with the storm as his accompanist, he stood and began to play—the Kreutzer Sonata of Beethoven.

The moments passed, moments that were days in the creation of that world of fire and stars; abysses and heights of passionate struggle, the idea of order, and the resolution of these in the greatness of the human spirit. Never before had Rudolf played with such mastery—or with such an accompanist. Waves and wind beat the tower with giant hands. Steadily above them the beacon blazed in its sure cycles of darkness and light. The last note ceased and Rudolf dropped his head on his chest, breathing hard. The ocean seethed over the island with a roar as of many voices.

The old man had sat unmoving through the work, his broad gnarled hands resting on his thighs, his head bowed, listening massively. For some time he continued to sit in silence. Then he looked up, lifted those hands calmly, judiciously, and nodded his head.

"Yes," he said. "That is true."

Just as the wave cannot exist for itself
But must always participate in the swell of the ocean,
So we can never experience our lives by ourselves
But must always share the experiencing of life that takes
place all around us.

But there is only one thing that has power
Completely, and that is love.
Because when a man loves,
He seeks no power
And therefore he has power.

—Alan Paton

From a poster by Sister Mary Corita Kent, attributed to Alan Paton.

Insecurity

For if we think of this existence of the individual as a larger or smaller room, it appears evident that most people learn to know only a corner of their room, a place by the window, a strip of floor on which they walk up and down. Thus they have a certain security. And yet that dangerous insecurity is so much more human which drives the prisoners in Poe's stories to feel out the shapes of their horrible dungeons and not be strangers to the unspeakable terror of their abode. We, however, are not prisoners. No traps or snares are set about us, and there is nothing which should intimidate or worry us. We are set down in life as in the element to which we best correspond, and over and above this we have through thousands of years of accomodation become so like this life, that when we hold still we are, through a happy mimicry, scarcely to be distinguished from all that surrounds us. We have no reason to mistrust our world, for it is not against us. Has it terrors, they are our terrors; has it abysses, those abysses belong to us; [when there] are dangers at hand, we must try to love them. And if only we arrange our life according to that principle which counsels us that we must always hold to the difficult, then that which now still seems to us the most alien will become what we most trust and find most faithful. How should we be able to forget those ancient myths that are at the beginning of all peoples, the myths about dragons that at the last moment turn into princesses; perhaps all the dragons of our lives are princesses who are only waiting to see us once beautiful and brave. Perhaps everything terrible is in its deepest being something helpless that wants help from us.

—Rainer Maria Rilke

. . . My heart is a stupid bird
   whose country is the void
 whose food
  is the blue of the sky
   and if any hand in the world
    tried
  to build him a cage,
   before it could set in place
   the second bar
it would have killed my bird.

My heart
   is any airy boat
drawn always somewhere else
 and if any hand in the world
   tried to bring it to harbour,
  it would fold its red sail
 as a well-behaved guest
folds his napkin after dinner,
  then it would bow
  and allow itself
  to sink.

My heart
   is only a cloud
drawn to the big storms
     and if any hand in the world
     tried one day to seize it
the hand would very soon feel
   like a shuddering wing
an eyelid
       or a heart
or perhaps only a clock
     in the end one never
        knows
        but
when the hand opened again
   from the cloud
     there would only remain,
to crown with light
   the five candles of flesh,
   a drop of rain
enclosing
      the dancing fiery bridle
     of a rainbow.

—Minou Drouet (8 years old)

25

Freedom

A pair of swallows would not fly well with their wings bonded to each other. Watch them. They soar and dive, sometimes close, sometimes far apart, freely sharing the space bctwccn them and around them. Without that space, what life would they have? It must be nice, too, to huddle together in the dark, or on a stormy day, with visions of flying still tingling in their small warm bodies.

—SA

If you love something,
    Set it free.
If it comes back to you,
    It's yours.
If it doesn't,
    It never was.

—(SU)

Companionship

All companionship can consist only in the strengthening of two neighboring solitudes, whereas everything that one is wont to call giving oneself is by nature harmful to companionship: for when a person abandons himself, he is no longer anything, and when two people both give themselves up in order to come close to each other, there is no longer any ground beneath them and their being together is a continual falling.

Once the realization is accepted that even between the *closest* human beings infinite distances continue to exist, a wonderful living side by side can grow up, if they succeed in loving the distance between them which makes it possible for each to see the other whole and against a wide sky.

—Rainer Maria Rilke

Reprinted from RILKE ON LOVE AND OTHER DIFFICULTIES by John J.L. Mood, with the permission of W.W. Norton & Company, Inc., Copright 1975 by W.W. Norton & Company, Inc.

Human Love

Whoever looks seriously at it finds that neither for death, which is difficult, nor for difficult love has any explanation, any solution, any hint or way yet been discerned; and for these two problems that we carry wrapped up and hand on without opening, it will not be possible to discover any general rule resting in agreement. . . .

We are only just now beginning to look upon the relation of one individual person to a second individual objectively and without prejudice, and our attempts to live such associations have no model before them. And yet in the changes brought about by time there is already a good deal that would help our timorous novitiate.

The girl and the woman, in their new, their own unfolding, will but in passing be imitators of masculine ways, good and bad, and repeaters of masculine professions. After the uncertainty of such transitions it will become apparent that women were only going through the profusion and the vicissitude of those (often ridiculous) disguises in order to cleanse their own most characteristic nature of the distorting influences of the other sex. Women, in whom life lingers and dwells more immediately, more fruitfully and more confidently, must surely have become fundamentally riper people, more human people, than easygoing man, who is not pulled down below the surface of life by the weight of any fruit of his body, and who, presumptuous and hasty, undervalues what he thinks he loves. This humanity of woman, borne its full time in suffering and humiliation, will come to light when she will have stripped off the conventions of mere femininity in the mutations of her outward status, and those men who do not yet feel it approaching today will be surprised and struck by it. Some day (and for this, particularly in the northern countries, reliable signs are already speaking and shining), some day there will be girls and women whose name will no longer signify merely an opposite of the masculine, but something in itself, something that makes one think, not of any complement and limit, but only of life and existence: the feminine human being.

This advance will (at first much against the will of the outstripped men) change the love-experience, which is now full of error, will alter it from the ground up, reshape it into a relation that is meant to be of one human being to another, no longer of man to woman. And this more human love (that will fulfill itself, infinitely considerate and gentle, and kind and clear in binding and releasing) will resemble that which we are preparing with struggle and toil, the love that consists in this, that two solitudes protect and border and salute each other.

—Rainer Maria Rilke

29

be of love(a little)
More careful
Than of everything
guard her perhaps only

A trifle less
(merely beyond how very)
closely than
Nothing,remember love by frequent

anguish(imagine
Her least never with most
memory)give entirely each
Forever its freedom

(Dare until a flower,
understanding sizelessly sunlight
Open what thousandth why and
discover laughing)

—e.e. cummings

Abou Ben Adhem

Abou Ben Adhem (may his tribe increase!)
Awoke one night from a deep dream of peace,
And saw, within the moonlight in his room,
Making it rich, and like a lily in bloom,
An angel writing in a book of gold.
Exceeding peace had made Ben Adhem bold,
And to the presence in the room he said,
    "What writest thou?"—The vision rais'd its head,
And with a look made of all sweet accord,
Answer'd, "The names of those who love the Lord."
    "And is mine one?" said Abou. "Nay, not so,"
Replied the angel. Abou spoke more low,
But cheerly still; and said, "I pray thee, then,
Write me as one that loves his fellow men."
    The angel wrote, and vanish'd. The next night
It came again with a great wakening light,
And show'd the names whom love of God had blest,
And lo! Ben Adhem's name led all the rest.

—Leigh Hunt

31

Doing Good

Many years ago I was invited by an Air Force psychiatrist to come up to his base and teach the staff a little about Gestalt Therapy. After my talk, Bill told me about his dissatisfactions with life in the military. He talked about the salary and all the benefits that kept him there, and all the rules and restrictions that bothered him. At one point he said, "I pay a terrible price for all those benefits." I, just wanting to be friendly, said, "Well, I guess we all have our price," meaning that we all make difficult choices and compromises in a less-than-perfect world, and that benefits seldom come to us without some kind of "price."

Much later, by chance, I learned that my simple comment somehow led Bill to carefully examine the price he was paying, and to decide that he didn't want to pay it any more. Since he had just signed up for another 3-year hitch, he couldn't just quit. So he faked a psychotic depression, palmed and flushed the drugs they gave him, and was discharged soon after, free to find a new life with a different price.

I know there have also been many times when a simple comment by someone else has changed the direction of my life—and how many others were there that I didn't even notice?

Robert Fulghum writes about a sufi story in which God decides to reward a good man by granting him a wish. The man wished to do good for others without knowing about it. And God decided that it was such a good wish that he would grant it to everyone.*

—SA

*I have not been able to find the original story; I will appreciate any information that would help me track it down.

Praying

Ann Landers once paraphrased Blaise Pascal as follows:

> "If there is no God, we have nothing to lose by praying, and if there is one, we have much to lose if we don't."

My response is that if God is half as omniscient and understanding as s/he is supposed to be, then:

1. S/he will not be much impressed by the sincerity of Pascal's sort of praying, and,

2. S/he will understand (better than I) why I am not a believer.

On the other hand, if God is not omniscient and understanding, there probably isn't much point in praying to God anyway.

However, belief in God and in the value of prayer would not be so widespread if it didn't have some value. Even if there is no God, praying may still be very, very useful to the person who prays. Different religions pray in different ways, of course. However, here are a few of the ways in which praying can be useful.

Foremost, it can provide a sense of connection with something much larger and more enduring that ourselves, a respite from the separation and transience that so many of us often feel.

Praying can also be a meditative opportunity, a quiet time to pause to reground and recenter ourselves. Temporarily withdrawing from the hectic struggles of everyday life, we can refocus on the "why" of it all, and reconnect with the deeper values that make our lives worth living. What is truly important to us? What do we want to be doing with our lives?

Giving thanks and blessings to others makes it easier to forgive and accept them, and it also creates an attitude of giving out of ourselves that returns to bless us, nourishing us, refreshing us, and healing us—and creating a private sanctuary which we can return to in our dark hours. Gratitude for what has been given to us can be a reminder that most of what we have has little to do with our efforts, but is unmerited blessing.

Asking for guidance can open me to the wisdom of my inner knowing—the voices, visions and feelings that embody this knowing, valuable guides that are so often ignored in the rush and confusion of daily activities and the demands of others. Asking for guidance can also open me to all the messages available to me in the world around me that I have been ignoring.

—SA

Who rises from prayer a better man, his prayer is answered.

—George Merideth

Asking

As a dirt-poor graduate student at Brandeis University in the late 1950's, I often walked along the nearby Charles River. Much of the shoreline was undeveloped woods, but one area was dotted with large homes, set in broad lawns sloping down to boat docks. At one of these docks there was always an aluminum canoe, upside down to keep out the rain. Time after time I imagined enjoying paddling that canoe along the river.

Finally one day I put my imagination to somewhat better use; I imagined walking up to the door of the house and asking if I could use it. I also went on to imagine the probable refusal and the disappointment I would feel. After several days of doing this, I went even further to imagine the much less likely alternative—that the canoe's owner might agree to let me use it. With *both* alternatives in mind, I could compare them. On the one hand, almost certain probability of refusal and a few moments of disappointment. On the other hand, the very slim chance of agreement, and hours and hours of canoeing pleasure. Looking at it this way I had a great deal to gain, and very little to lose, so I walked up to the door and knocked.

Much to my surprise, the people who owned the canoe actually welcomed my request. They had often thought about how little they used the canoe, and wished that more people could enjoy it. I enjoyed canoeing often during the rest of that summer, and the next summer as well, exploring the river for miles both upstream and down.

Since then I have explored many other unlikely possibilities—especially when it took very little effort, and the possible benefit was large. Most of these yielded nothing in return, but the few that did made it well worthwhile. Ask not, and you get not; ask, and you shall receive—at least some of the time.

—SA

Deserving

Most people think they deserve something if they worked hard for it, or if they want it very badly, or if they have the money to buy it. And often they use this "deserving" as a reason why someone else should give them something.

However, the only relevant factor in "deserving" something is being able to appreciate it. If you can fully appreciate something, then you deserve it.

I don't deserve a bottle of fine wine—even though I could buy it—because I don't enjoy wine. Even if I bought it and drank it, I wouldn't *really* have it, because it would mean nothing to me. That would truly be casting "pearls before swine."

But if I can appreciate a painting, I deserve it because I respond to it and find it beautiful. And because I can appreciate it, I can truly have it fully, even when I can't buy it and own it.

If you want to deserve things, learn to appreciate them, and they will be yours.

> —SA, with thanks to Leslie LeBeau,
> who taught me about deserving.

"Do" List

Mend a quarrel
Seek out a forgotten friend
Write a love letter
Share some treasure
Give a soft answer
Encourage youth
Keep a promise
Find the time
Give something away
Throw something out
Forgive an enemy
Listen
Apologize if you were wrong
Apologize even if you weren't
Think first of someone else
Be kind and gentle
Laugh a little
Laugh a little more
Express your gratitude
Gladden the heart of a child
Take pleasure in the beauty and wonder of the earth
Speak your love
Speak it again
Speak it still once again

—(AU)

Art

There are many kinds of art, of course; one of my favorites is painting. I certainly don't know what "good" art is—and I don't think the "art experts" know either. Clearly what is considered to be "good" or "great" art—like what is considered to be "good manners"—varies enormously from age to age, and from one culture to another. Most million-dollar paintings would not bring five dollars at a yard sale without an identifying signature.

I can only tell you that I respond to some paintings in lasting ways, and say a little about what that does for me. First, I find that the art I enjoy nourishes me. Although it's not quite a substitute for food, I have actually sometimes gone to a museum or gallery hungry, and after looking at some paintings literally felt full and no longer hungry for a while. When I am tired and tense, I can pause to look around at the paintings and photographs in my home and find myself relaxing, breathing more deeply, invited out of my limited world and into one that is expansive and full-filling. I can also do the same thing with the memories of paintings in my mind. In fact, I have found that sometimes when I see a painting again it is not as beautiful as I remember it! Somehow my mind responded to the painting's invitation by changing it and improving it.

The art that I like most has just enough vagueness and uncertainty that my eyes and mind have to work a little to put it all together, insisting that I participate in the process. This uncertainty means that I see it a little differently each time I look at it, keeping it forever fresh and new, promising more perspectives yet to be discovered.

The art that I love also always teaches me something about the world, by emphasizing or pointing out something that I hadn't seen before. When gazing at a painting I often find myself realizing "Yes, that *is* the way the shadows fall across a snowbank." "That's *just* the way that plum branches bend and twist." "That *is* exactly the way that sunlight breaks through the lingering clouds after a storm." After Monet, water lilies cannot look the same, because my mind is forever colored by Monet's brush strokes. After Van Gogh, who can look at sunflowers or a starry night with the same eyes?

So I seek out the art that nourishes me and teaches me, usually in ways that are far beyond the words I have to describe it.

—SA

Things are not all so comprehensible and expressible as one would mostly have us believe; most events are inexpressible, taking place in a realm which no word has ever entered, and more inexpressible than all else are works of art, mysterious existences, the life of which, while ours passes away, endures.

—Rainer Maria Rilke

Reprinted from LETTERS TO A YOUNG POET by Rainer Maria Rilke, translated from the German by M. D. Herter Norton, with the permission of W. W. Norton & Co., Inc. Copyright 1934 by W. W. Company, Inc., renewed 1962 by M. D. Herter Norton. Revised edition copyright 1954 by W. W. Norton & Company, Inc.

Giving Thanks

There is a story of an old farmer in the 1860s whose land lay along the western migration route in the Midwest. Since the small stream that ran through his farm was the only water along that section of the route, emigrants usually stopped their dusty wagons under the old cottonwood trees to water their horses and cool and rest for awhile, listening to the refreshing sounds of the tumbling water and the summer insects echoing softly in the deep shade. Those who reached the stream late in the day would often camp there overnight before continuing their trek westward.

After all his chores were finished in the evening, the old farmer would often walk down the sloping fields to the stream to visit these emigrants. He liked to talk with them, listening to the sounds of the night and to see if there was some small thing he could do to ease their westward journey.

The old farmer's slow, measured manner and his soft, deep voice put even frightened children at ease quickly and most people were eager to visit with him. His deeply wrinkled face reminded them of the furrowed bark of the cottonwood trees and his eyes sparkled like the little stream where it tumbled in the sunlight over a rock or a small branch. He seemed as much a part of the land as the green and yellow lichen-covered boulders along the creek, left there by the glaciers some fifteen thousand years before.

The old farmer would often talk with his visitors about what he knew of the trail ahead, suggesting pleasant places to rest or warning of difficult stretches. Sometimes he would take a few raisins out of his faded overalls, carefully brush the blue lint off them with his gnarled fingers and give them to a fussy child to soothe him and allow the child's tired mother to get some sleep.

At other times, he would reach into his overalls for a nail, a screw, or a scrap of leather to mend something broken in their wagon. Sometimes he would bring along a few cherries or apricots from his small orchard, some fresh green beans from his garden or some other small treat to brighten their spirits at the end of the day.

When he found travelers on the verge of despair, he would reach into his overall bib and produce letters that were falling apart from many foldings and unfoldings and read from them slowly by the flickering light of a kerosene lamp. These letters were from previous travelers who wrote eagerly of finding a new home somewhere in the vast wilderness ahead and of their simple pleasures as they began to settle down and create a new life for themselves. The words from these letters fell on the weary travelers like a spring rain, refreshing and nourishing their spirits.

At times, one of the travelers would think of settling nearby and would ask about the people in that region. To these inquiries the old farmer would always reply, "Well, tell me about the people where you come from."

Sometimes the traveler's face would harden, especially around the mouth, and he would reply, "Oh, it was terrible back there. No one could get along with anyone else. People were mean and gossipy, judgemental and self-righteous. There was always some dispute over land or who should fix a fence; I couldn't wait to get out of there and finally I told my wife we had to leave."

Upon hearing this, the old farmer would frown slightly and say, "Well, you know, you'd find the people around here just like that. You'll probably want to move on in the morning."

At other times a traveler thinking of settling in the area would reply wistfully, "Oh, we loved it at home. We had so many friends; everyone helped each other through the hard times. We got together for barn-raising after the fall harvest, sharing what little we had. When our neighbor broke his leg one spring, we all pitched in to plant his fields for him, and when we were hailed out one year, he gave us grain for the winter and seed corn for the next spring. We really hated to leave, but my wife and I started to think about the space and opportunities out West and the new friends we would meet, so we decided to move on."

When he heard this, the old farmer's smile seemed to become as broad as a Kansas sunrise in the summertime, and he would say, "Well, you know, you'd find the people around here just like that. Why don't you rest up a day or two and look around at some of the land that's available nearby. I'd be happy to show you around and introduce you."

—Steve Andreas

I first heard this story from my high school science teacher E.R. Harrington in 1955. He probably adapted it from the following poem:

The Right Kind of People

Gone is the city, gone the day,
Yet still the story and the meaning stay:

Once where a prophet in the palm shade basked
A traveler chanced at noon to rest his miles.
"What sort of people may they be," he asked,
"In this proud city on the plains o'erspread?"
"Well, friend, what sort of people whence you came?"
"What sort?" the packman scowled; "why, knaves and
fools."
"You'll find the people here the same," the wise man said.

Another stranger in the dusk drew near,
And pausing, cried "What sort of people here
In your bright city where yon towers arise?"
"Well, friend, what sort of people whence you came?"
"What sort?" the pilgrim smiled,
"Good, true and wise."
"You'll find the people here the same,"
The wise man said.

—Edwin Markham

From POEMS OF EDWIN MARKHAM, SELECTED AND ARRANGED by
CHARLES L. WALLIS. Copyright 1950 by Virgil Markham. Copyright renewed.
Reprinted by permission of HarperCollins Publishers, Inc.

Live the Questions

. . . be patient toward all that is unsolved in your heart and to try to love the *questions themselves* like locked rooms and like books that are written in a very foreign tongue. Do not now seek the answers, which cannot be given you because you would not be able to live them. And the point is, to live everything. Live the questions now. Perhaps you will then gradually, without noticing it, live along some distant day into the answer.

—Rainer Maria Rilke

Reprinted from LETTERS TO A YOUNG POET by Rainer Maria Rilke, translated from the German by M. D. Herter Norton, with the permission of W. W. Norton & Co., Inc. Copyright 1934 by W. W. Norton & Company, Inc., renewed 1962 by M. D. Herter Norton. Revised edition copyright 1954 by W. W. Norton & Company, Inc.

Pleasure

Physical pleasure is a sensual experience no different from pure seeing or the pure sensation with which a fine fruit fills the tongue; it is a great unending experience, which is given us, a knowing of the world, the fullness and the glory of all knowing. And not our acceptance of it is bad; the bad thing is that most people misuse and squander this experience and apply it as a stimulant at the tired spots of their lives and as distraction instead of a rallying toward exalted moments.

—Rainer Maria Rilke

Reprinted from LETTERS TO A YOUNG POET by Rainer Maria Rilke, translated from the German by M. D. Herter Norton, with the permission of W. W. Norton & Co., Inc. Copyright 1934 by W. W. Norton & Company, Inc., renewed 1962 by M. D. Herter Norton. Revised edition copyright 1954 by W. W. Norton & Company, Inc.

Heaven and Hell

The old monk sat by the side of the road. With his eyes closed and his legs crossed and his hands folded in his lap, he sat. In deep meditation, he sat.

Suddenly his zazen was interrupted by the harsh and demanding voice of a samurai warrior. "Old man! Teach me about Heaven and Hell!"

At first, as though he had not heard, there was no perceptible response from the monk. But gradually, he began to open his eyes, the faintest hint of a smile playing around the corners of his mouth as the samurai stood there waiting . . . impatient . . . growing more and more agitated with each passing second.

"You would know the secrets of Heaven and Hell?" replied the monk at last. "You who are so unkempt. You whose hands and feet are covered with dirt. You whose hair is uncombed, whose breath is foul, whose sword is all rusty and neglected. You who are ugly and whose mother dresses you funny. *You* would ask me of Heaven and Hell?"

An excerpt from "A Proper Hell," published in the July-September 1994 issue of *Christian*New Age Quarterly* (PO Box 276, Clifton, NJ 07011-0276).

The samurai uttered a vile curse. He drew his sword and raised it high above his head. His face turned to crimson, the veins on his neck stood out in bold relief as he prepared to sever the monk's head from its shoulders.

"That is Hell," said the old monk gently, just as the sword began its descent.

In that fraction of a second, the samurai was overcome with amazement, awe, compassion, and love for this gentle being who had dared to risk his very life to give him such a teaching. He stopped his sword in mid-flight and his eyes filled with grateful tears.

"And that," said the monk, "is Heaven."

—Father John W. Groff, Jr.

Tears

It is not widely recognized that there are several different kinds of tears. Once, many years ago, when I was very far from "civilization," a tooth started aching slightly. Thinking it was the result of yet another sinus infection, I didn't do anything about it. It gradually worsened, and when I realized that something ought to be done about it, it was already the start of a long 3-day weekend. More and more frequent aspirins only dulled the throbbing pain a little; Monday morning found me on the doorstep of the nearest dentist. After an x-ray, the dentist determined that the tooth should come out. He gave me a shot of novocaine and let me rest while it took effect. As the tides of pain began to recede, I was flooded with a feeling of relief, and tears poured down my face. A nurse looked in and asked worriedly if I was all right. I replied that I felt *wonderful!* So there are tears of relief.

People are most familiar with tears of sadness or loss. Often when people cry it is because someone or something that they had, or hoped to have, was taken away. Tears of grief acknowledge the importance of what has been lost, and the resulting feeling of emptiness.

There are also tears of reunion, when someone or something returns to us, and we rejoin with what has been lost. These tears of connection arise out of a sense of fullness, or even an overflowing of fullness.

There are also tears of thanks or gratitude, when we welcome an experience that is beyond our hopes or expectations. These may be quite similar—perhaps identical—to tears of reunion, except that we usually don't have a prior sense of loss—it's just that something happens that suddenly fills us with a sense of unexpected fullness.

A few years ago, in early spring, I was following other cars along a slushy street. The car ahead splashed muddy water up onto a snowbank where a cluster of bright yellow daffodils were blooming through the snow. Something in that snapshot of life blossoming gloriously through adversity touched me, and I had the thought "Another spring; I didn't know I'd get another one." Tears and a strong feeling of gratitude and happiness welled up in me—thankfulness for what is, in that moment.

A mystic friend I have known for over 30 years has told me that the "gift of tears" has been known as a spiritual path for a long time. Seeking out, remembering, cultivating, and treasuring experiences that make us cry in this way can develop gratefulness that goes beyond those moments to become an attitude that pervades all living. Although I haven't attained it, it makes sense to me that ultimately one could have an attitude of gratefulness for every moment—no matter how disturbing or painful—and that this would be a good and useful way to live.

Gratitude is not only the greatest of virtues, but the parent of all the others.

—Cicero

One single grateful thought raised to heaven
is the most perfect prayer.

—G. E. Lessing

There is yet another aspect of this "gift of tears." Often these tears express a sense of a simple, yet deep, abiding, and pervasive truth, typically a truth not fully honored or appreciated in our day-to-day living. These truths can only be hinted at with words, and certainly can't be captured by them. The truth is evident in being touched deeply, and the tears often make it difficult or impossible to speak any words at all. It may be that these tears of truth are actually the same as tears of gratitude and reunion—that in all these experiences we reunite with something that we didn't even know we were separated from, something infinitely great and eternally true and wonderful that we can catch a glimpse of now and then.

—SA

Tears are often the telescope by which men see far into the heaven.

—Henry Ward Beecher

A Tale For All Seasons

"Tell me the weight of a snowflake," a coal-mouse asked a wild dove.

"Nothing more than nothing," was the answer.

"In that case, I must tell you a marvelous story," the coal-mouse said.

"I sat on the branch of a fir, close to its trunk, when it began to snow—not heavily, not in a raging blizzard—no, just like in a dream, without a sound and without any violence. Since I did not have anything better to do, I counted the snowflakes settling on the twigs and needles of my branch. Their number was exactly 3,741,952. When the 3,741,953rd dropped onto the branch, nothing more than nothing, as you say—the branch broke off."

Having said that, the coal-mouse flew away.

The dove, since Noah's time an authority on the matter, thought about the story for awhile, and finally said to herself, "Perhaps there is only one person's voice lacking for peace to come to the world."

—Kurt Kauter

New Fables, Thus Spoke "The Carabou" by Kurt Kauter.

53

Thanks

Her name was Fran. She lived with her family upstairs above the apartment that three of us had rented during our senior year of college. She was in her last year of high school, going through the same struggles and uncertainties that most of us have at that time of life. We sort of became "uncles" to her, offering friendly points of view that were somewhat different—and considerably less demanding—than those of her parents and her boyfriend. Then we graduated, moved out, and went our separate ways.

I had taken a job not too far away, and on a return visit I heard that Fran's parents had kicked her out of her house. I found her in a rooming house, totally lost, without friends or a job or car or any idea what to do next. As we talked, I found out that as part of a high school typing course she had taken a proficiency exam and also a county civil service exam. I made a couple of phone calls, drove her to the county employment offices, and found a job for her. This lifted Fran's spirits considerably, but now she was overwhelmed by the prospect of traveling 20 miles to work without a car. So I got bus schedules and we figured out how she could get there. It still looked like a pretty long and complicated trip, but I explained to her that since it was a large office she could ask around and probably soon find someone who lived near her to car pool with.

When I checked in with her a week later, she was a totally different person. She glowingly told me that she had found someone to car pool with on the first day, the job was going well, and she was also making some new friends at work. Her happiness was palpable, but what I will always remember is her overwhelming gratitude for the little things I had done to help her. That gratitude was a far greater gift than my small help.

—SA

I am done with great things and big plans, great institutions and big success. I am for those tiny, invisible loving human forces that work from individual to individual, creeping through the crannies of the world like so many rootlets, or like the capillary oozing of water, which, if given time, will rend the hardest monuments of pride.

—William James

Mending Wall

Something there is that doesn't love a wall,
That sends the frozen-ground-swell under it
And spills the upper boulders in the sun,
And makes gaps even two can pass abreast.
The work of hunters is another thing:
I have come after them and made repair
Where they have left not one stone on a stone,
But they would have the rabbit out of hiding,
To please the yelping dogs. The gaps I mean,
No one has seen them made or heard them made,
But at spring mending-time we find them there.
I let my neighbor know beyond the hill;
And on a day we meet to walk the line
And set the wall between us once again.
We keep the wall between us as we go.
To each the boulders that have fallen to each.
And some are loaves and some so nearly balls
We have to use a spell to make them balance:
"Stay where you are until our backs are turned!"

We wear our fingers rough with handling them.
Oh, just another kind of outdoor game,
One on a side. It comes to little more:
There where it is we do not need the wall:
He is all pine and I am apple orchard.
My apple trees will never get across
And eat the cones under his pines, I tell him.
He only says, "Good fences make good neighbors."
Spring is the mischief in me, and I wonder
If I could put a notion in his head:
"Why do they make good neighbors? Isn't it
Where there are cows? But here there are no cows.
Before I built a wall I'd ask to know
What I was walling in or walling out,
And to whom I was like to give offense.
Something there is that doesn't love a wall,
That wants it down." I could say "Elves" to him,
But it's not elves exactly, and I'd rather
He said it for himself. I see him there,
Bringing a stone grasped firmly by the top
In each hand, like an old-stone savage armed.
He moves in darkness as it seems to me,
Not of woods only and the shade of trees.
He will not go behind his father's saying,
And he likes having thought of it so well
He says again, "Good fences make good neighbors."

The Loyal Soldier

During World War II, at the height of Japanese expansion in the Pacific, there were Japanese garrisons on literally thousands of tiny islands scattered across an enormous cxpansc of occan. When the tide of battle turned, many of these were overrun and defeated, but some were entirely missed. On other islands, small groups of soldiers or isolated survivors hid in caves in inaccessible areas. A few years later, the war was over. But since these survivors didn't know this, they continued to struggle, maintaining their rusting weapons and tattered uniforms as best they could, totally isolated, yearning to be reunited with their command.

In the years immediately following the war, many of these soldiers were discovered when they shot at fishermen or tourist boats, or were found by natives. As the years passed, these discoveries became less frequent. The last one was some thirty years after the war had ended.

Consider the position of such a soldier. His government had called him, trained him, and sent him off to a jungle island to defend and protect his people against great external threat. As a loyal and obedient citizen, he had survived many privations and battles through the years of war. When the ebb and flow of battle passed him by, he was left alone or with a few other survivors. During all those years, he had carried on the battle in the best way he could, surviving against incredible odds. Despite the heat, the insects, and the jungle rains, he carried on, still loyal to the instructions given to him by his government so long ago.

How should such a soldier be treated when he is found? It would be easy to laugh at him, and call him stupid for continuing to fight a war that had been over for thirty years.

Instead, whenever one of these soldiers was located, the first contact was always made very carefully. Someone who had been a high-ranking Japanese officer during the war would take his old uniform and samurai sword out of the closet, and take an old military boat to the area where the lost soldier had been sighted. The officer would walk through the jungle, calling out for the soldier until he was found. When they met, the officer would thank the soldier, with tears in his eyes, for his loyalty and courage in continuing to defend his country for so many years. Then he would ask him about his experiences, and welcome him back. Only after some time would the soldier gently be told that the war was over, and that his country was at peace again, so he would not have to fight anymore. When he reached home he would be given a hero's welcome, with parades and medals, and crowds thanking him and celebrating his arduous struggle and his return and reunion with his people.

—Connirae and Steve Andreas
(with thanks to Greg Brodsky)

Stranger

Stranger, do not come one step nearer
do not reach out toward me
stranger
we must not touch our hands
to join your loneliness and mine

Abide by the regulation:
       no man shall approach a man
       no woman shall approach a woman
       nor man, woman, nor woman, man
Our life depends on it

You wear a red scarf
I wear a blue cap
there can be nothing between us

If you ask me the time, I must turn my wrist
If I ask you the way, you must point

The rules hang from every lamppost
above the basket of geraniums
they are nailed into the telephone poles

From *Journey Through the Light,* p.10. © 1973, Peter Goblen, Koheleth Publishing Co., San Francisco CA.

Though we scream to break the silence
who would conjecture the universality of his sorrow
who would confess at the streetcorner

Stranger, at the time of fire
        you will pass through the smoke to save me
Stranger, at the time of flood
        I will lift you from the water
At the time of the invader
        we will gather together

Guard us from our intimacy
now, as we stand adjacent on the endless belt
conveying us into the future
which, like the ancients' heaven
will justify the disaster of this hour

—Peter Goblen

when serpents bargain for the right to squirm
and the sun strikes to gain a living wage—
when thorns regard their roses with alarm
and rainbows are insured against old age

when every thrush may sing no new moon in
if all screech-owls have not okayed his voice
—and any wave signs on the dotted line
or else an ocean is compelled to close

when the oak begs permission of the birch
to make an acorn—valleys accuse their
mountains of having altitude—and march
denounces april as a saboteur

then we'll believe in that incredible
unanimal mankind(and not until)

—e.e. cummings

Man is the only animal that blushes. Or needs to.

—Mark Twain

At Harvesttime

There is an immutable life principle with which many people will quarrel.

Although nature has proven season in and season out that if the thing that is planted bears at all, it will yield more of itself, there are those who seem certain that if they plant tomato seeds, at harvesttime they can reap onions.

Too many times for comfort I have expected to reap good when I know I have sown evil. My lame excuse is that I have not always known that actions can only re-produce themselves, or rather, I have not always allowed myself to be aware of that knowledge. Now, after years of observation and enough courage to admit what I have observed, I try to plant peace if I do not want discord; to plant loyalty and honesty if I want to avoid betrayal and lies.

Of course, there is no absolute assurance that those things I plant will always fall upon arable land and will take root and grow, nor can I know if another cultivator did not leave contrary seeds before I arrived. I do know, however, that if I leave little to chance, if I am careful about the kinds of seeds I plant, about their potency and nature, I can, within reason, trust my expectations.

—Maya Angelou

From WOULDN'T TAKE NOTHIN' FOR MY JOURNEY NOW by Maya Angelou. Copyright © 1993 by Maya Angelou. Reprinted by permission of Random House, Inc.

Complaining

When my grandmother was raising me in Stamps, Arkansas, she had a particular routine when people who were known to be whiners entered her store. Whenever she saw a known complainer coming, she would call me from whatever I was doing and say conspiratorially, "Sister, come inside. Come." Of course I would obey.

My grandmother would ask the customer, "How are you doing today, Brother Thomas?" And the person would reply, "Not so good." There would be a distinct whine in the voice. "Not so good today, Sister Henderson. You see, it's this summer. It's this summer heat. I just hate it. Oh, I hate it so much. It just frazzles me up and frazzles me down. I just hate the heat. It's almost killing me." Then my grandmother would stand stoically, her arms folded, and mumble, "Uh-huh, uh-huh." And she would cut her eyes at me to make certain that I had heard the lamentation.

At another time a whiner would mewl, "I hate plowing. That packed-down dirt ain't got no reasoning, and mules ain't got good sense. . . . Sure ain't. It's killing me. I can't ever seem to get done. My feet and my hands stay sore, and I get dirt in my eyes and up my nose. I just can't stand it." And my grandmother, again stoically with her arms folded, would say, "Uh-huh, uh-huh," and then look at me and nod.

As soon as the complainer was out of the store, my grandmother would call me to stand in front of her. And then she would say the same thing she had said at least a thousand times, it seemed to me. "Sister, did you hear what Brother So-and-So or Sister Much to Do complained about? You heard that?" And I would nod. Mamma would continue, "Sister, there are people who went to sleep all over the world last night, poor and rich and white and black, but they will never wake again. Sister, those who expected to rise did not, their beds became their cooling boards, and their blankets became their winding sheets. And those dead folks would give anything, anything at all for just five minutes of this weather or ten minutes of that plowing that person was grumbling about. So you watch yourself about complaining, Sister. What you're supposed to do when you don't like a thing is change it. If you can't change it, change the way you think about it. Don't complain."

It is said that persons have few teachable moments in their lives. Mamma seemed to have caught me at each one I had between the age of three and thirteen. Whining is not only graceless, but can be dangerous. It can alert a brute that a victim is in the neighborhood.

—Maya Angelou

Dedication

The storm had been raging for many days. The ground everywhere was covered with broken branches, and there was so much water it was hard to tell what was creek and what was land, except for the sounds of the rushing waters. For days the mother bird had huddled over her three babies, her wings partly spread, sheltering them from the driving rain, each gust of wind threatening to tear her little nest from the frantically lurching branches. But now the water was rising steadily, the higher waves splashing droplets onto the mother as she huddled.

She realized that soon her nest would be swept away, and they would all be drowned. She also realized that she could only carry one of her babies in her tiny claws. What was she to do? She picked up one of her babies and started to fly through the storm, across the rising water, seeking some place that would be high enough, so that she might save at least one of her children.

As she flew, she spoke to her baby, asking, "When I am very old and I can no longer take care of myself, will you dedicate your whole life to taking care of me, just as

A Traditional Yiddish Tale, Set down by Stanley A. Leichtling

I am using all my energy and strength to take care of you now?"

Her baby turned to her and said, "No. When your day has passed, when you can no longer take care of yourself, then I will not dedicate my whole life to taking care of you. I will dedicate all my energy and strength to taking care of myself."

The mother bird thought to herself, "No! This is not the baby to save." She let go of it, and sadly watched as it fell, helplessly flailing its tiny wings, into the muddy waves below.

Tired and wet, she turned and flew back to her nest, which she hoped would still be above the swiftly rising waters.

She picked up another baby and flew off again through the beating rain and the driving wind, seeking a place that would be high enough, so she might save at least one of her children.

As she flew, she spoke to the second baby, asking the same question, "When I am very old and I can no longer take care of myself, will you dedicate your whole life to taking care of me, just as I am using all my energy and strength to take care of you now?"

Her baby looked at her and said, "Yes. When you have used all your energy and strength, when you are too exhausted to go further, I will dedicate my whole life to taking care of you."

The mother bird thought, "No! This also is not the baby to save." She let go of her baby and again watched sadly as the small body fluttered helplessly, flailing its tiny wings, until it was swallowed by the rushing waters below.

Summoning all her remaining strength, she again turned and flew back to her nest. Just before the turbulent waves reached her nest, she picked up her third baby and flew away again. With barely enough strength to rise above the foam and spray, driven by the howling wind, she struggled bravely on, desperately seeking a place that would be high enough, so she might save the last of her children.

As she struggled, with her voice and body failing, she spoke to her baby, asking, "When I am very old and I can no longer take care of myself, will you dedicate your whole life to taking care of me, just as I am using all my energy and strength to take care of you now?"

Her baby turned to her and said softly, "No. When you have used all your energy and strength, when you are too exhausted to go further, I will not dedicate my whole life to taking care of you. I will dedicate all my strength and energy to taking care of my children, just as you are taking care of me now." The mother felt a strong and vibrant "YES" course throughout her body, giving her renewed hope and strength, as she struggled on through the wind and rain.

Living Fully

I would like all of us to live as fully as we can. The only time I really feel awful is when people have not lived a life that expressed themselves. They lived with all their "shoulds" and "oughts" and their blaming and placating and all the rest of it, and I think, "How sad."

—Virginia Satir

And I suppose that before I leave this world, one thing that I would wish for all the world to know, is that human contact is made by the connection of skin, eyes, and voice tone. These are the things that taught us before we had words. How our parents touched us, how they looked at us, what their voices sounded like, were all recorded in us.

Human contact is not about words. Human contact is about eye connection, about voice, about skin, about breathing. Words are something you can read in a book, you can see on a billboard, and they can be totally differentiated from human beings. Words help when people are congruent.

—Virginia Satir

The Yes/No Medallion

As one way of communicating to people that their own experiences, whatever they were, were valid, in themselves, and did not require any explanation or justification, Virginia Satir often asked them to visualize a medallion made of something wonderful to them, to hang around their necks:

On one side is written "No." And under "No" it says, "Thank you for noticing me, but what you ask doesn't fit for me right now, so the answer is No."

And you turn it over, and on the other side it says "Yes." And then it says, "Thank you for noticing me. What you asked me fits wonderfully well, and the answer is Yes."

And then when you get timid at a certain point in time, you take out your medallion and you put the one side out that really fits. And then you look underneath, and you know what to say.

—Virginia Satir

The Sultan's Perfect Tree
by Jane Yolen

There was once a sultan who loved perfection. In his palace he would allow only the most perfect things. Each fruit that he ate had to be without blemish. Each cup that he drank from had to be without flaw. The servants who waited upon him were always handsome or beautiful, with features set exactly in their faces, and limbs not an inch too long or short. Everything, in fact, was perfect.

One day in the fall, the sultan was looking out at his perfect garden. Seven gardeners saw to it that only the most beautiful plants were allowed to grow. Every morning they would trim off broken branches or dying leaves and replace any flower that was in danger of drooping.

In the center of the garden grew a tree. It had been planted by the grandfather of the sultan and was tall and straight and kept perfectly shaped.

As the sultan gazed out his window at the garden, his eyes most naturally fell on the tree at its center. Suddenly, a swift wind blew into the garden, more savage than any wind before it. The tree bowed and swayed, its leaves shaking and shivering, turning up first the red side, then the gold. As the sultan watched, many of the leaves were ripped loose from their stems and blown to the ground. Soon the tree looked patchy, as if painted in by a trembling hand.

"It is not perfect," the sultan said angrily to himself. Then more loudly he cried out, *"It is not perfect!"*

At his cry, the servants came running. "What is it, O perfect one," they asked, for so they had been instructed to address him.

"That!" the sultan answered angrily, pointing out the window at the offending tree.

"It is but a tree," said the newest serving girl, daughter of the chief steward. Though she was beautiful to look at, she was not yet perfect in her conduct.

"But it is no longer perfect," said the sultan. "I want a perfect tree. A perfect autumn tree."

"How is that to be done?" inquired the chief steward, for he knew well enough to let the sultan give instructions.

"Call the gardeners!" ordered the sultan.

The seven gardeners came at a run. They caught the falling leaves in willow baskets and carried them out of sight. They plucked the remaining leaves from the tree, climbing to the top on shaky wooden ladders. But they were not quick enough for the sultan.

He turned away from the window and cried, "It is *not perfect.* Take down the tree."

The chief steward was so shocked, he forgot for a moment to be perfect. "But it is your grandfather's tree," he stammered. "It was planted on the day your father was born."

And because his grandfather had been perfectly wise in all that he did, the sultan said, "Then I shall not cut it down."

"What shall be done, then?" asked the chief steward, once again the perfect servant.

"Close up my window to the garden," said the sultan. "And send for the best painter in my kingdom. Have him paint me a perfect autumn tree on a screen. Set the screen before the window. Then when I let my gaze fall that way, I shall always see a perfect tree."

So it was done. The best painter in the kingdom was sent for. He labored seven days until he had painted a magnificent autumn tree, upright, tall, and completely red-gold.

"Perfect," said the sultan when the painter was done.

Two servants set the screen before the window and the painter was rewarded handsomely.

For several months the sultan was delighted. Often he would remark to his chief steward, "*There* is a perfect autumn tree."

Meanwhile, outside it had grown cold. The winter snows came swirling down from the far mountains. All around, the world lay still and white—everywhere but on the sultan's autumn tree.

One day, as the sultan sat drinking his tea, the newest young serving girl came into the room. She carried a bowl in which winter branches were perfectly arranged and set in hard-packed snow.

"O perfect master," she said, "pray accept this representation of the season."

The sultan looked from the bowl to the screen, where his perfect autumn tree stood, splendid and red-gold. His face grew thoughtful. Then it grew angry.

"My tree is no longer perfect!" the sultan cried out. "For if it were, it would be blanketed in snow."

At his cry, the other servants came running, the chief steward in the lead. "What is it, O perfect one?"

"That!" the sultan said angrily, pointing to the screen.

"But that is your perfect autumn tree," said the young serving girl, with only the hint of a smile on her face.

"Perfect autumn tree, yes," said the sultan. "But now it is winter."

"Do not be upset, O perfect master," said the chief steward. "We shall make it perfect."

Again the painter was summoned and he labored yet another seven days to paint a perfect winter tree on another panel of the screen, a tree that was blanketed with snow.

And for several months the sultan was delighted with his perfect winter tree.

But while the sultan gazed with satisfaction at his tree, the world outside had begun to change once more. Little shoots of green were pushing through the brown cover of earth. The trees were wearing buds like delicate green beads.

One day as the sultan sat deep in thought, the young serving girl again entered the room, this time bearing a vase with branches that were covered with young buds and tender green leaves.

"What is this, child?" asked the sultan.

"O perfect master," she said, "pray accept the gardeners' gift of the season."

Again the sultan saw that his tree was no longer perfect, and he cried out in anger. Again the chief steward summoned the painter to paint a new scene. And again, for a few months the sultan was happy.

But one day, as the sultan sat in perfect contentment, the young servant girl brought him yet another vase filled with fully green boughs and ripe fruit. As she moved toward the table, the branches in the vase bobbed and swayed with their burden.

Neither the sultan nor the girl exchanged a word this time, but when she had gone, the sultan looked over at the screen, his heart heavy in his breast. With several sharp claps of his hand, he called the chief steward to him.

"The tree on my screen is no longer perfect," the sultan said sadly. "It is not fully green and laden with fruit. It does not bend and sway with the weight of its burden. Its imperfection rests heavily on my heart," he confided. "I will not eat or drink until I have a perfect tree."

The chief steward sent for the painter at once. "The tree you painted is no longer perfect," he explained. "This time, our perfect sultan requires a tree that will bend and sway with the weight of its ripe fruit. Only then will it be perfect."

The painter looked downcast. "What you ask, alas, I cannot do. I am a painter, not a god. With my paints, I can make a perfect tree—perfect *for the moment*. But I cannot make it live. I cannot make it grow. I cannot make it change."

Then what shall we do?" cried the chief steward, as much to himself as to the painter. He sat down by the sultan's great canopied bed and wept, his face in his hands.

"If we cannot make a perfect tree, the sultan will not eat or drink. And if he does not eat or drink, he will surely waste away and die."

The painter sat down by his side and wept likewise, for he loved the perfect sultan and did not wish to see him waste away and die.

One by one, as they heard the weeping, the serving men and women came into the room, listened to the sad tale, and sat down beside the chief steward and cried. Soon there was a whole row of them, sitting and sighing and weeping for want of a perfect tree.

At last the new young serving girl came in and saw the rows of weeping servants. When she, too, had heard the tale, she said, "Oh, you perfect sillies! I know how to make such a tree. It is perfectly simple."

"How can you know," the chief steward asked his daughter sharply, "when the sultan who is the perfect master, the painter who is the perfect painter, and we who are the perfect servants do not know?"

"Perhaps it is because I am not yet perfect," said the young girl, "For to be perfect means the end of growing. Close your eyes and you shall see."

They all did as they were told—even the chief steward—and the young serving girl went over to the window. Carefully, she took down the folding screen. Outside, the real tree at the garden's center was covered with fruit, and, with every passing breeze, its leaves fluttered and its branches bent and bowed.

"Now you may open your eyes," she said.

The servants opened their eyes and gazed at the place where the screen had been. They saw out into the garden and looked upon the real tree. "Oh!" they all cried.

The chief steward and the painter opened their eyes and saw the tree. "Aah!" they both sighed.

At that, the sultan opened his eyes. He sat up in his bed. Slowly, he rose and went over to the window. For a long, long time he gazed out at the tree. He saw how some of the branches were nearly full and some nearly empty. He saw how some of the branches were short and some long. He saw how some of the branches were almost all green and how some were almost all brown.

"It is not perfect," he said softly.

The servants began to murmur worriedly. The chief steward looked over at his daughter, an angry scowl beginning to crease his handsome brow. But the sultan cut all this short with a wave of his hand.

"It is not perfect," he said, "but it is living, and growing, and changing. That is better than perfect!"

Then he took the young serving girl by the hand and, together, they went out of the palace into the garden to enjoy the fruit of the tree.

Fear

Nasrudin was walking along a lonely road one moon-lit night when he heard a snore, somewhere, it seemed, underfoot. Suddenly he was afraid, and was about to run when he tripped over a dervish lying in a cell which he had dug for himself, partly underground.

"Who are you?" stammered the Mulla.

"I am a dervish, and this is my contemplation-place."

"You will have to let me share it. Your snore frightened me out of my wits, and I cannot go any further tonight."

"Take the other end of this blanket, then," said the dervish without enthusiasm, "and lie down here. Please be quiet, because I am keeping a vigil. It is a part of a complicated series of exercises. Tomorrow I must change the pattern, and I cannot stand interruption."

Nasrudin fell asleep for a time. Then he woke up, very thirsty.

"I am thirsty," he told the dervish.

"Then go back down the road, where there is a stream."

"No, I am still afraid."

"I shall go for you, then," said the dervish. After all, to provide water is a sacred obligation in the East.

Reprinted by permission from *The Exploits of the Incomparable Mulla Nasrudin* by Idries Shah (Octagon Press Ltd, London).

"No—don't go. I shall be afraid all by myself."

"Take this knife to defend yourself with," said the dervish.

While he was away, Nasrudin frightened himself still more, working himself up into a lather of anxiety, which he tried to counter by imagining how he would attack any fiend who threatened him.

Presently the dervish returned.

"Keep your distance, or I'll kill you!" said Nasrudin.

"But I am the dervish," said the dervish.

"I don't care who you are—you may be a fiend in disguise. Besides, you have your head and eyebrows shaved!" The dervishes of that order shave the head and eyebrows.

"But I have come to bring you water! Don't you remember—you are thirsty!"

"Don't try to ingratiate yourself with me, Fiend!"

"But that is my cell you are occupying!"

"That's hard luck for you, isn't it? You'll just have to find another one."

"I suppose so," said the dervish, "but I am sure I don't know what to make of all this."

"I can tell you one thing," said Nasrudin, "and that is that fear is multidirectional."

"It certainly seems to be stronger than thirst, or sanity, or other people's property," said the dervish.

"And you don't have to have it yourself in order to suffer from it!" said Nasrudin.

—Idries Shah

Scattershot

Never believe them. Receive my words, my dear,
as the world seals up man's campsite scar, as air
accepts the air-age, as time endures its clocks.
I speak as a pouting child throws aimless rocks,
as a dog snarls at a wheel; my bullets flare
from a soldier raking the jungle night—for fear.

—Judson Jerome

From *Light in the West* by Judson Jerome, p.18. Reprinted by Permission, Golden Quill Press, Manchester Center, VT.

Crabs

If you were to leave a burlap bag,
bunching and clicking, full of live crabs,
on the beach, tied at the top, stuffed
with shifting shells inside its sag,
each sticky stalk-eye blind and tender,

claws pinching claws—or nothing—clacking,
hard, hollow bodies scraping as
legs worked them through the bodies, backing,
you would know how full of things I lie,
dry, out of reach of the folding sea,

inert and shapeless, were it not
for rattling crabs inside of me
that hear, perhaps, the long waves crushing,
the flute of the wind through grass and sand,
remember the water, the cool salt hushing,

struggle to slit the burlap and
scatter in sideways, backwards courses,
like beetles, devils, flat as clocks—
these snapping wants, these shelled remorses—
to drag themselves beneath the rocks.

—Judson Jerome

From *Light in the West* by Judson Jerome, p.19. Reprinted by Permission, Golden Quill Press, Manchester Center, VT.

Muddy Road

Tanzan and Ekido were once traveling together down a muddy road. A heavy rain was still falling.

Coming around a bend, they met a lovely girl in a silk kimono and sash, unable to cross the intersection.

"Come on, girl," said Tanzan at once. Lifting her in his arms, he carried her over the mud.

Ekido did not speak again until that night when they reached a lodging temple. Then he no longer could restrain himself. "We monks don't go near females," he told Tanzan, "especialy not young and lovely ones. It is dangerous. Why did you do that?"

"I left the girl there," said Tanzan. "Are you still carrying her?"

—Paul Reps

From *Zen Flesh, Zen Bones: A collection of Zen and pre-Zen writings,* compiled by Paul Reps. © 1957 Charles E. Tuttle Company, Inc.

The Troubled Squirrel

Once upon a time, or twice down within a time, there was a very troubled ground squirrel. His troubles were not simple ones, like his fear when the shadow of a hawk swept across the ground nearby, or when a coyote's yelp split the night. Nor was his pain like the ache of an injured leg, for at all those times he knew what to do or what not to do.

Often he felt very young and very, very small; at other times he felt very old, and bone-weary. But mostly he felt confused, and frustrated, and very lost. When he thought about his troubles, it was as if he were at the shady side of the pond in the meadow, groping in the muddy water for a slippery bottom-dweller. At times he would feel a tantalizing touch within his grasp, and seem to be at the brink of understanding, before it slithered away into the swirling gloom.

At other times his troubles were like a cloud, muting the colors around him and casting a dark shadow over all his days. Yet when he searched the heavens for the source of this shadow, the wide blue sky gave him no answer.

Sometimes his troubles seemed like soft voices, as if just out of reach, and he strained his ears to hear what meaning they might reveal to him. But always it was only a breeze or a large insect rattling the stems of the dry grasses or the leaves over his head.

After much thought and anguish, his mind turned to the many stories he had heard of the oldest and wisest squirrel who, it was said, lived alone in the deepest burrow in the meadow. All the stories about the old squirrel were curious and puzzling, full of strange twists and unpredictable behavior. Some said the the old squirrel was wise beyond imagining, while others said that he was crazy, or worse. Others said he was both, but there was no telling one from the other. When he thought of all these stories his mind swirled with images, sounds and feelings that reached no resolution.

At last, one evening when the weight of his troubles pressed down particularly heavily upon his shoulders, he decided to seek out the wise old squirrel, come what may. As he slowly descended to deeper and deeper levels, the activities of the other squirrels and the sounds of their comings and goings gradually faded away. As he crept though these burrows where the dust and dampness had not been disturbed—for who knows how long—the sound of his soft breathing and his footfalls echoed in the long-abandoned chambers. Sometimes when he paused, he thought he could hear the gentle heartbeat of the earth itself.

As he explored burrows he had never visited before, in some he found only cobwebs and old nests made of leaves and twigs, the hulls of nuts and seeds, and other signs of the life that had once occupied them. In others he found the walls sparkling with tiny grains of some shiny crystal that he had never encountered in the shallower burrows nearer the surface. In yet others he found fragile patterns of roots and spiderwebs that seemed to welcome him and beckon him deeper and deeper.

As the soft light faded into almost total darkness, he seemed at the same time to be traveling deeper and deeper into himself, into unseen and unheard realms that began to whisper soft and poignant meanings to him.

Eventually he reached a level where only one burrow still angled downward. It was a large burrow, free of dust and cobwebs, and the smell and warmth of life radiated from its walls, a little like the sound of a soft choir in a great cathedral. As he reached the end of this burrow and his eyes slowly adjusted to the darkness, he saw before him an immense squirrel whose eyes were closed, and whose fur was almost completely white with age. Without opening its eyes, the great white squirrel muttered, "What do you want?" As the troubled squirrel began to pour out his misery, he was astonished to feel his unhappiness empty out of him as cleanly as if he were a pants pocket that someone had turned inside out to see what was there, spilling its contents out into the sunlight where they could be seen clearly. It seemed as if the old squirrel was picking through the jigsaw puzzle of his life with gentle, loving hands, carefully separating pieces that had been jammed together, and rearranging and uniting pieces that had been long been separated, simply curious to see what image would slowly emerge from the scattered bits of color.

He remembered a time when he was much younger, watching other squirrels playing in the pond, fascinated by the fragmented reflections flashing on the surface of the water. And when the squirrels left the water, watching the scattered dancing bits of light slowing their dance and gradually coalescing into larger patterns of color and shape, until finally he saw an image of himself, still moving. And as he watched this image of himself slowly move toward stillness, he felt the calmness of the quieting water enter his body and refresh him.

After what seemed to be an eternity, the great white squirrel's eyes opened and he began to hum a soft low sound. As he gazed into these eyes, he felt a comfort and safety he had never known before, and he seemed to be drawn into the heart of life itself. He felt himself welcomed to slide into their depths and into a peaceful reverie in which he lost all track of time.

In this timeless realm some of his thoughts seemed like soap bubbles riding within a gentle breeze, until they popped and vanished, while others gradually became so tangible that they seemed to pervade throughout all space and time, and through every fiber of his being.

At the same time, the myriad sounds of his nature rose and fell around him and gradually become a quiet, yet joyous song that conveyed the courage and majesty of his simple life. Tiny imperceptible movements—like tiny eager minnows swimming in his body releasing tensions into fluid movement, told him that his body too, was participating fully in this joyous learning, changing, rearranging.

These movements, images, and sounds stirred each other to greater searching and expression, and gradually melded into a subtle dance that resonated with every particle of his being, a moving that he would carry reverently in his body to the end of his days.

Some time later, as he found himself crawling slowly upward through the burrows, he felt a new lightness that told him that so much had changed in a delightfully solid way, though exactly what it was, or how it had happened, he couldn't begin to describe.

—SA

Rights

I have always been amused by those who protest restrictions on their "God-given" rights. Surely if their rights were given by God no one could take them away! The only God-given rights I know of are to live a certain span of time and then to die.

Rights are established by groups of people who want to make it easier or safer for people to be able to do certain kinds of things, . . . and to *not* do other kinds of things. But even agreements, rules, and laws don't actually establish rights; they only provide unpleasant consequences for violations of rights.

Many years ago Fritz Perls was speaking and demonstrating Gestalt Therapy in a high-school auditorium. With "no smoking" signs on every wall, Fritz chain-smoked throughout the whole two-hour talk. At the end, a woman walked up to him self-righteously and asked "How come you have the right to smoke in this school building?"

Fritz replied "I don't have the right, and I don't not have the right; I just do it."

—SA

87

How Nasrudin Created Truth

"Laws as such do not make people better," said Nasrudin to the King; "They must practice certain things, in order to become attuned to inner truth. This form of truth resembles apparent truth only slightly."

The King decided that he could, and would, make people observe the truth. He could make them practice truthfulness.

His city was entered by a bridge. On this he built a gallows. The following day, when the gates were opened at dawn, the Captain of the Guard was stationed with a squad of troops to examine all who entered.

An announcement was made: "Everyone will be questioned. If he tells the truth, he will be allowed to enter. If he lies, he will be hanged."

Nasrudin stepped forward.

"Where are you going?"

"I am on my way," said Nasrudin slowly, "to be hanged."

Reprinted by permission from *The Exploits of the Incomparable Mulla Nasrudin* by Idries Shah (Octagon Press Ltd, London).

"We don't believe you!"

"Very well, if I have told a lie, hang me!"

"But if we hang you for lying, we will have made what you said come true!"

"That's right: now you know what truth is—YOUR truth!"

—Idries Shah

If a man will begin with certainties, he shall end in doubts; but if he will be content to begin with doubts, he shall end in certainties.

—Francis Bacon

If a little knowledge is dangerous, where is the man who has so much as to be out of danger?

—T. H. Huxley

Metaphysics

One day a man was walking along a road, and instead of looking at the beautiful sky he was watching the pavement as he went along. Then he saw in the distance something very brilliant. He went rapidly towards it, picked it up and looked at this extraordinary thing, and he was in a state of beatitude, because it was extraordinarily beautiful. So he looked at it and put it in his pocket.

Behind were two people, also walking. One of them says to the other, "What was it that he picked up? Did you see his expression? What an ecstasy he was in by the very act of looking at it!" And the other—who happened to be the Devil—said, "What he picked up was truth." And the friend said "That is a very bad business for you that he has found it." The Devil replied, "Not at all. I am going to help him to organize it."

—(SU)

90

What! Out of nothing
    to provoke
A conscious something
    to resent the yoke
Of unpermitted pleasure
    under pain
Of everlasting penitance
    if broke?

—Omar Khayyam

From *The Rubiat* (Edward Fitzgerald)

On a metaphysician: A blind man in a dark room—
looking for a black hat—which isn't there.

—Lord Bowen

The Universe

I have heard a lot of discussion about whether the universe is friendly or not (toward *us,* that is). If I had to choose between the two, of course I'd prefer that it were friendly. And in the absence of a definitive answer, I'd prefer to *think* of it as friendly, even if it isn't—it just feels better to live that way.

However, if I review the information that astronomers and physicists have amassed, it doesn't appear to me that the universe is the slightest bit friendly toward life. Most of the universe is much too hot, or much too cold to even *permit* life, much less be friendly toward it.

Of the nine planets around our sun, only ours supports life (though it's possible that Mars once did for a while). Earth seems like a happy exception to the universe's apparent antipathy toward life. However, every 65 million years or so the universe throws a large asteroid at the earth, killing off from 50% to 90% of all species. And the history of other stars indicates that in another 10 billion years or so the Sun will explode and vaporize any life that might remain on our planet.

Although most people don't realize it, there could also be some problems if the universe is friendly toward life.

If the universe were actively fostering life, then the next question is "*Which* life would be favored?" Although we would like to believe that we would be the "chosen" life-form, this is a biased view and not a foregone conclusion. How would the universe decide which life to promote (at the expense of other forms of life)? And how might these preferences change with time? A friendly universe could be as capricious and fickle in its favors as the Greek Gods.

There is a third alternative to the universe being friendly or not; perhaps it just doesn't care at all! At first this might seem to be bad news for us, but I think it's *good* news. In an impartial universe, we can discover what regularities underlie the magnificent diversity around us, and figure out what we need to do to maintain our life and improve on it. All forms of life, and our human scientific enterprise, have been amazingly successful in discovering these impartial regularities—the "rules of the game"—and exploiting them to our advantage.

In an impartial universe we are without help, yes; but also without hindrance. We're on our own. Good luck to us.

—SA

The chess-board is the world; the pieces are the phenomena of the universe; the rules of the game are what we call the laws of Nature. The player on the other side is hidden from us. We know that his play is always fair, just, and patient. But also we know, to our cost, that he never overlooks a mistake, or makes the smallest allowance for ignorance.

—T. H. Huxley

Pusher

Beware the seeker of disciples
the missionary
the pusher
all proselytizing men
all who claim they have found
the path to heaven.

For the sound of their words
is the silence of their doubt.

The allegory of your conversion
sustains them through their uncertainty.

Persuading you, they struggle
to persuade themselves.

They need you as they say you need them:
there is a symmetry they do not mention
in their sermon
or in the meeting
near the secret door.

From *Journey Through the Light,* p.6. © 1973, Peter Goblen, Koheleth Publishing Co., San Francisco CA.

As you suspect each one of them
be wary also of these words,
for I, dissuading you,
obtain new evidence
that there is no shortcut,
no path at all,
no destination.

—Peter Goblen

Ignorance

The greatest fool may ask more questons that the wisest man can answer.
                              —Charles Caleb Colton

Two things are infinite: The Universe, and human stupidity—but I'm not sure about the universe.

                              —Albert Einstein

When a stupid man is doing something he is ashamed
of, he always declares that it is his duty.

                              —George Bernard Shaw

Ignorance, power, and pride are a deadly mixture.

                              —Robert Fulghum

From *All I Really Need to Know I Learned in Kindergarten,* by Robert Fulghum.
Copyright © 1986, 1988 by Robert Fulghum. Reprinted by permission of Villard
Books, a division of Random House, Inc.

Scholarship

Logic is an organized way of going wrong with confidence.

—Karl Popper

Scholarship is the process by which butterflies are transmuted into caterpillars.

—Jerry A. Fodor

From *The Modularity of Mind*, MIT Press, 1983.

The great tragedy of science—the slaying of a beautiful hypothesis by an ugly fact.

—T. H. Huxley

Truth

All great truths begin as blasphemies.

—George Bernard Shaw

It is the customary fate of new truths to begin as here-sies and to end as superstitions.

—T. H. Huxley

Error is none the better for being common, nor truth the worse for having lain neglected.

—John Locke

Truth is only the most expedient error.

—Hans Vaihinger

From *The Philosophy of As If*

The truth is always friendly.

—(SU)

Conation

Perhaps the paths of snails may be
A wasted effort marked by slime,
But I, too, bear the shell of me
That hinders and protects my climb.

Through cycles of uncertainties
We blindly grope and slowly crawl
Up awful cracks in theories
Or fissures in a garden wall.
                    —Robert Lee Brothers

From *Robert Lee Brothers: The Collected Poems* edited by Susan Ford Wiltshire, Ph.D. (in preparation).

99

Not truth, nor certainty. These I foreswore
In my novitiate, as young men called
To holy orders must abjure the world.
"If . . . , then . . . ," this only I assert;
And my successes are but pretty chains
Linking twin doubts, for it is vain to ask
If what I postulate be justified,
Or what I prove possess the stamp of fact.

Yet bridges stand, and men no longer crawl
In two dimensions. And such triumphs stem
In no small measure from the power this game,
Played with the thrice-attenuated shades
Of things, has over their originals.
How frail the wand, but how profound the spell!

—Clarence R. Wylie Jr.

From "The Imperfections of Science" by Warren Weaver. *Proceedings of the American Philosophical Society,* Vol. 104, No. 5, October, 1960.

Thought

Thought, I love thought.
But not the jiggling and twisting of
    already existent ideas
I despise that self-important game.
Thought is the welling up of known
    life into consciousness
Thought is the testing of statements
on the touchstone of the conscience
Thought is the gazing into the face of
    life, and reading what can be read,
Thought is pondering over
experience, and coming to
conclusion.
Thought is not a trick, or an exercise,
    or a set of dodges
Thought is a man in his wholeness
    wholly attending.

—D.H. Lawrence

"Thought" by D. H. Lawrence, from THE COMPLETE POEMS OF D.H. LAWRENCE by D. H. Lawrence, Edited by V. de Sola Pinto & F. W. Roberts. Copyright © 1964, 1971 by Angelo Ravagli and C. M. Weekley, Executors of the Estate of Frieda Lawrence Ravagli. Used by permission of Viking Penguin, a division of Penguin Books USA Inc.

Intelligence

What made this brain of mine, do you think? Not the need to move my limbs; for a rat with half my brains moves as well as I. Not merely the need to do, but the need to *know* what I do, lest in my blind efforts to live I should be slaying myself.

—George Bernard Shaw,
"Man and Superman"

One man that has a mind and knows it, can always beat ten men who haven't and don't.
—George Bernard Shaw

Good judgement comes from experience;
Experience comes from poor judgement.

(Found on a door at the Computing Center, University of Hawaii)

The Boilermaker

There is an old story of a boilermaker who was hired to fix a huge steamship boiler system that was not working well. After listening to the engineer's description of the problems and asking a few questions, he went to the boiler room. He looked at the maze of twisting pipes, listened to the thump of the boiler and the hiss of escaping steam for a few minutes, and felt some pipes with his hands. Then he hummed softly to himself, reached into his overalls and took out a small hammer, and tapped a bright red valve, once. Immediately the entire system began working perfectly, and the boilermaker went home. When the steamship owner received a bill for $1,000 he complained that the boilermaker had only been in the engine room for fifteen minutes, and requested an itemized bill. This is what the boilermaker sent him:

For tapping with hammer:	$.50
For knowing where to tap:	999.50
Total:	$1,000.00

—SA

(With gratitude to my high school science teacher, E.R. Harrington, who told me this story in 1952.)

Mistakes

When I was ten years old, my mother took me to a
county fair in British Columbia. Like most kids that age, I
begged for money to play all the games and win prizes. All
afternoon I threw darts at balloons, and balls at stacked
metal milk bottles, and played other "games of skill." At the
end of the day, as I looked at my little pile of tiny beer mugs
and cheap stuffed animals, my mother said quietly, "That
cost twenty-five dollars"—quite a lot of money in 1945.

That same summer I was captivated by ads in Outdoor
Life magazine for the Northwestern School of Taxidermy,
offering a correspondence course in stuffing animals. By
pumping our water cistern full for a dime and running er-
rands for a nickel, I slowly accumulated ten dollars and
paid for the course. As the instructions began to arrive, I
quickly realized that although the course cost only $10,
the tools, preservatives, paint, glass eyes, and other mate-
rials needed to complete it were going to cost a great deal
more. I successfully stuffed one small bird before I gave
up. The lesson was clear to me, and my mother didn't
need to say anything this time.

My mother had a philosophy about making mistakes
that went like this: You can't avoid making mistakes, but

you do have some choices about *when* you make them. You can make small mistakes when you're young, or big mistakes when you're older. She let me make many more mistakes than most parents did, and considered the expense a good investment. It took a few more experiences like this before I fully learned to be cautious and thoughtful about apparent opportunities: "A fishing lure doesn't have to catch a fish; it only has to catch a fisherman."

—SA

If something is worth doing,
It's worth doing badly at first.

(SU)

Rules make the learner's path long, examples make it short and successful.

—Seneca

Examining Life

"The unexamined life is not worth living."

—Socrates

"The unlived life is not worth examining."

—SA

The only point in knowing *about* experience is if it helps me to have fewer of the kinds of experiences I don't like and more of the experiences I do like. The rest of the time, experience itself is the point.

—SA

The mystery of life is not a problem to be solved, but is a reality to be experienced.

—J.J. Van der Leeuw

Maturity

"Maturity is doing what you want to do even when your mother thinks it's a good idea."

—Paul Watzlawick

Once someone asked Paul Watzlawick how to determine when couple therapy could be terminated. He answered, "When the couple is having breakfast, and the husband says, 'This coffee is terrible,' and they both know that he is talking about the coffee."

—SA

The world was made for fools.
Their reckless laughter leaps the facts
And acts
Ere passion cools.

Were but the wise as brave!
Their ponderous judgments wait for speech
Till each
Is in his grave.

Then call the fools the wise.
They're better fitted to the earth
With mirth
Than wisdom's sighs.

—Warren S. McCulloch

From *Embodiments of Mind,* p. 332. © 1965, MIT Press, Cambridge MA.

Controlled Folly

A man of knowledge lives by acting, not by thinking about acting, nor by thinking about what he will think when he has finished acting. A man of knowledge chooses a path with heart and follows it; and then he looks and rejoices and laughs; and then he *sees* and knows. He knows that his life will be over altogether too soon; he knows that he, as well as everybody else, is not going anywhere; he knows, because he *sees,* that nothing is more important than anything else. In other words, a man of knowledge has no honor, no dignity, no family, no name, no country, but only life to be lived, and under these circumstances his only tie to his fellow men is his controlled folly. Thus a man of knowledge endeavors, and sweats, and puffs, and if one looks at him he is just like any ordinary man, except that the folly of his life is under control. Nothing being more important than anything else, a man of knowledge chooses and acts, and acts it out as if it matters to him. His controlled folly makes him say that what he does matters and makes him act as if it did, and yet he knows that it doesn't; so when he fulfills his acts he retreats in peace, and whether his acts were good or bad, or worked or didn't is in no way part of his concern.

—Carlos Casteneda

From Carlos Casteneda, *The Teachings of Don Juan: A Yaqui Way of Knowledge.* Copyright © 1968 The Regents of the University of California.

Ladle Rat Rotten Hut

Wants pawn term, dare worsted ladle gull hoe lift wetter murder inner ladle cordage honor itch offer lodge dock florist. Disc ladle gull orphan worry ladle cluck wetter putty ladle rat hut, end fur disc raisin pimple colder ladle rat rotten hut. Wan moaning rat rotten hut's murder colder inset: "Ladle rat rotten hut, heresy ladle basking winsome burden barter end shirker cockles. Tick disc ladle basking tudor cordage offer groin murder hoe lifts honor udder site offer florist. Shaker lake, dun stopper laundry wrote, end yonder nor sorghum stenches dun stopper torque wet strainers."

"Hoe-cake, murder," resplendent ladle rat rotten hut, end tickle ladle basking an stuttered oft. Honor wrote tudor cordage offer groin murder, ladle rat rotten hut mitten anomalous woof.

"Wail, wail, wail," set disc wicket woof, "evanescent ladle rat rotten hut! Wares or putty ladle gull goring wizard ladle basking?"

"Armor goring tumor groin murder's," reprisal ladle gull. "Grammars seeking bet. Armor ticking arson burden barter end shirker cockles."

From *Word Study*, XXVIII, no. 5 (May, 1953), 4. (AU)

"O hoe! Heifer blessing woke," setter wicket woof, butter taught tomb shelf, "Oil tickle shirt court tudor cordage offer groin murder. Oil ketchup wetter letter, an den—O bore!"

Soda wicket woof tucker shirt court, end whinney retched a cordage offer groin murder, picket inner widow an sore debtor pore oil worming worse lion inner bet. Inner flesh disc abdominal woof lipped honor betting adder rope. Zany pool dawn a groin murder's nut cup an gnat gun, any curdle dope inner bet.

Inner ladle wile ladle rat rotten hut a raft attar cordage an ranker dough ball. "Comb ink, sweat hard," setter wicket woof, disgracing is verse. Ladle rat rotten hut entity bet rum end stud buyer groin murder's bet. "O grammar," crater ladle gull, "Wart bag icer gut! A nervous sausage bag ice!" "Buttered lucky chew whiff, doling," whiskered disc ratchet woof, wetter wicket small. "O grammar, water bag noise! A nervous sore suture anomalous prognosis!" "Buttered small your whiff," inserter woof, ants mouse worse waddling. "O grammar, water bag mousey gut! A nervous sore suture bag mouse!"

Daze worry on forger nut gull's lest warts. Oil offer sodden throne offer carvers end sprinkling otter bet, disc curl and bloat Thursday woof ceased pore ladle rat rotten hut an garbled erupt.

Mural: Yonder nor sorghum stenches shut ladle gulls stopper torque wet strainers.

Problems

Life is just one damn thing after another. The problem for people who come in to therapy is that life has become the same damn thing over and over again.

—John Weakland

Problems will always be with us. The problem is not the problem; the problem is the way people cope. This is what destroys people, not the "problem." Then when we learn to cope differently, we deal with the problems differently, and they become different.

—Virginia Satir

Life can only be understood backwards, but it must be lived forwards.

—Soren Kierkegaard

Life is thickly sown with thorns, and I know of no other remedy than to pass quickly through them.

—Voltaire

A great part of the happiness of life consists not in fighting battles, but in avoiding them.

—Henry Wadsworth Longfellow

I have a simple philosophy: Fill what's empty, Empty what's full, Scratch where it itches.

—Alice Rooseveldt Longworth

The Oak Beams of New College, Oxford

I owe this story to a man who was I think a New College student and was head of the Department of Medicine at the University of Hawaii, where he told it to me.

New College, Oxford, is of rather late foundation, hence the name. It was probably founded around the late 16th Century. (Oxford University was founded in the mid-12th Century, A.D.) It has, like other colleges, a great dining hall with big oak beams across the top, yes? These might be eighteen inches square, twenty feet long.

Some five to ten years ago, so I am told, some busy entomologist went up into the roof of the dining hall with a penknife and poked at the beams and found that they were full of beetles. This was reported to the College Council, who met in some dismay, because where would they get beams of that caliber nowadays?

One of the Junior Fellows stuck his neck out and suggested that there might be on College lands some oak. These colleges are endowed with pieces of land scattered

Reprinted from *CoEvolution Quarterly,* Summer 1976; subscriptions to *Whole Earth Review* are $20 a year (4 issues) from FULCO, 30 Broad St., Denville, NJ 07834, (800) 783-4903.

114

across the country. So they called in the College Forester, who of course had not been near the College itself for some years, and asked him about oaks.

And he pulled his forelock and said, "Well, sirs, we was wonderin' when you'd be askin'."

Upon further inquiry it was discovered that when the College was founded, a grove of oaks had been planted to replace the beams in the dining hall when they became beetly, because oak beams always become beetly in the end. This plan had been passed down from one Forester to the next for four hundred years. "You don't cut them oaks. Them's for the College 'all."

A nice story. That's the way to run a culture.

—Gregory Bateson

A Notebook Sketch for a Dream

The curtain opens on a poorly lit stage. A group of actors are waiting to try out for a play. Little groups are scattered over various parts of the stage and in the orchestra pit: They pantomime, deliver lines, and practice gestures, expressions and accents. From time to time they rest and try to impress each other. They all speak to each other—not conversation, but a cluster of monologues—as members of a competitive guild who must tolerate each other's company, and who never speak to anyone outside the guild unless it is to buy a pair of socks, or ask for a clean fork. Then again, through gossiping they may learn a new trick or gesture, or hear of a new play to try out for, or of someone's hard luck and a place they can fill. Their banter is a mixture of derogation and praise, always searching for something useful. None of them knows anything about the new play, and so everyone is practicing a number of different parts so they will not be at a loss. Each is sure that someone else must know something about the play, so all are constantly watching the others for a clue. If they only knew what the play was, they could practice the specialties required by the roles. As it is, they can only practice as many different parts as they can, in the hope that one of them may be useful.

116

As this is going on, a young man comes in from the rear of the darkened theater. He is strangely different from the actors, but not a striking figure in himself. He is not the sort one would ever notice immediately in a passing sidewalk crowd, or even at a party. He is the kind of person who seems to take form slowly before your eyes, as when you take your seat for a half-day's train ride and fail to notice anyone worthy of further interest. We always quickly scan those who surround us so that an inner voice may sigh with relief "safe," or perhaps "sit facing this way—that man has a strange look."

But then it may happen, and this is rare, that sometime later one finds oneself staring at a particular person, most often a girl, or a child perhaps—one seldom sees it in a man. And once you have startled yourself with this interest in a stranger, analysis begins, . . . and fails. You note details of face and expression, but still you are left with an aura of attraction and interest—something you cannot describe, nor find anywhere else in the sooty, smelly train. Still you wonder, but give up the attempt at analysis and instead relax and bathe in this pleasant feeling that you find in this unknown and yet known someone.

And as you relax, then perhaps comes the realization that it has never occurred to this person that she might be watched. You know, too, that if she knew, she would only smile back briefly in acknowledgement; nothing else would change. She would see in your look only you, not your reflection of her. She is and acts in the flow of her expanding into her surroundings—not conscious of her*self*, that sorry object that is rented to employers, but of her *living,* which even here is full of wonder and novelty. And you wonder, "How can she do this in this smoky, swaying car where even thought is as gritty as the blackened window sills?" And then suddenly you realize that you, too, have been exploring the wonder of life in this girl,

117

and you wonder "Has anyone ever looked at me? Did they ever see this?"

You look and you see again what you could not analyze before—her face is not a mask or a stage, but rather a window to the spirit. In you or I, an expression seems to be only a new layer which is sprayed upon the face, contorting the skin like a gesture in a well-planned play. In such a rare person, however, one can see what happens inside; one can see the feelings welling up from the depths. The face is only the outer limit of the powers of expression, not a painted cover to hide the rusty mechanisms behind.

An image flashes into mind. The grimy outer walls of adjacent apartment buildings, with rows of dirty windows—all but one with drawn shades. The one window is directly opposite me, and as I peek through a pinprick in my window shade, I see that this one window is clean and bright and open, with flowers on the sill, and colorful curtains at the sides. Startled and amazed, I step back and think, "Why, someone must live there! What a rare thing!" I try to look again, but I cannot see well, so I roll up my shade and rub some soot off the window with the heel of my hand. Still I cannot see, so I throw up the window and lean out into the air and sunshine. How strange and wonderful it is to see so clearly!

As the young man approaches the stage, all the people in the theater look curiously at him, trying to place him so that they will know how to act toward him.

Young man: I would like to be in this with you—
              may I?"

Actor 1:   But this is a play! Only actors can be in it.
              Are you an actor?

118

Actor 2:	What parts can you play?
Young man:	How can I tell until I'm in the play?
Actor 1:	Well, we don't know what the play is going to be, either, but that's not the question. You have to have a repertoire of roles in readiness for the tryout.
Young man:	But each time, each play, is new and different isn't it? How can I plan?
Actress 1:	Each play is a little different, but the parts are all established and decided upon. It is all arranged ahead of time.
Actress 2:	And the best actor is the one who can imitate the particular role best. The director won't stand for a performance that might alter his plans.
Actor 2:	What, can you do nothing? Come, show us what you can do—Here are some examples: (He acts first as an angry landlord, then as the young student who argues with him, then as the student's stuffy professor.)
Actor 1:	One never knows what part one may be called upon to play. You must always be ready with a few appropriate lines and gestures. It would be *wretched* if you had nothing to say!
Young man:	Sometimes I find that nothing is the best thing to say. But when I am *in* a situation, I always know what to do—or rather, I *do* it, and then glance back to see what I did if I'm curious. Every time it's new and different!

119

Actress 2:	(laughs) The director doesn't think so.
Actor 1:	Look, if you were in a play, how would *we* know what you were going to do?
Actress 1:	It's absurd! It's so much easier to know what to do—just watch for cues and memorize the lines.
Young man:	(sadly) But if you all did as I do...
Actor 2:	(happily) And if someone's sick or leaves, and an understudy takes their place, it makes no difference at all!
Actor 1:	Why do you want to be in the play? I'm afraid there's no place for you here until you've had some practice and learned some lines.

The Director comes out with some heavy scripts, and a stage hand carries out a placard which he places upside down on a stand. The sign reads: "Tryouts for a new play: LIFE." The young man stares sadly at them all for a few minutes and then walks slowly out.

—SA (1959)

Plans

What makes God laugh?
Hearing our plans.

(SU)

All our final decisions are made in a state of mind that is not going to last.

—Marcel Proust

Life is what happens to you while you're planning other things.

—John Lennon

Opinions

America's first bathtub was built in Cincinnati in 1842. Constructed of mahogany, lined with sheet lead, it was exhibited at a Christmas party. The next day the local newspapers denounced it as a "luxurious and democratic vanity." Doctors warned that the bathtub would be "a menace to health." The next year, in 1843, Philadelphia undertook by public ordinance to prohibit bathing between November 1 and March 15. Two years later Boston made bathing unlawful except when prescribed by a physician.

—Herbert V. Prochnow

From the book: THE COMPLETE TOASTMASTER, by Herbert V. Prochnow, © 1960.

There is no sin but ignorance.

—Christopher Marlowe

It is better to be stupid than hunchedback—it does not show.

—(Old German saying)

"Hand-feeding" of infants became the wisdom in England in the 18th century because King James II thought it was a good idea after several previous children had died while being wet-nursed. "Hand-feeding" meant replacing breast milk with "pap" made from animal milk, cereal, flour, sugar and spice, or "panada" made from broth, bread crumbs, and flavorings. From 1775 to 1800, 10,227 babies died at the Dublin Foundling Hospital—a mortality rate of 99.9%! These figures did not suggest to the hospital that they might be doing something wrong.

—Valerie Fildes

From BREASTS, BOTTLES AND BABIES by Valerie Fildes. Copyright © 1985 by Edinburgh University Press. Reprinted with permission of the publisher.

Once I hired several carpenters to build some homes and cabins on a ranch in Utah. One of them, Jim, had pretty strong opinions about just about everything. Just after we had been treated to yet another of Jim's diatribes, one of the other carpenters quietly said something that I have recalled many many times in the intervening twenty-five years: "There ain't hardly a thing, right or wrong, that Jim don't know."

—SA

Evil

Man, proud man,
Drest in a little brief authority,
Most ignorant of what he's most assur'd,
His glassy essence, like an angry ape,
Plays such fantastic tricks before high heaven,
As make the angels weep.

—William Shakespeare

A belief in a supernatural source of evil is not necessary; men alone are quite capable of every wickedness.

—Joseph Conrad

Good is better than evil
Because it is nicer.

—Mammy Yokum (Al Capp)

Evil is Live—backwards.

—(SU)

Anger

Think of the last time you got really angry, and reexperience what that was like.. . . .

Before you got angry, did you do the following: "Well, let's see, I could do this; I could do that; I could do the other thing. . . . No, I think I'll get angry instead."

In workshops and seminars I have asked literally thousands of people this question, and not a single person has said "Yes, that's how it was." We get angry when we're totally frustrated, when all the things we've tried haven't worked, and we're feeling trapped, and completely out of choices.

If you're already angry and haven't expressed it, it can help a lot to yell and beat up a pillow (as long as you don't inflict it on innocent bystanders). And in certain life-or-death situations, anger can mobilize the power to survive through violence. But in most situations, anger and violence are responses out of place, signs of weakness, not power.

The way to have less inappropriate anger in your life is to take the time to create many more choices for yourself—choices about how you think about things, choices about what else you could do, and choices about how you feel. With a wider range of choices, that trapped, out-of-choices, experience of frustration that provokes anger and violence will occur much less frequently.

—SA

125

Apologies

A few weeks ago I was driving on the freeway when I accidentally "cut off" someone who was coming off the entrance ramp. (I could also say that he was in a hurry and could have slowed a bit and entered traffic behind me, but let's assume I was at fault.) A few minutes later as he passed, he gave me a vigorous version of the middle-finger salute. I had no intent to anger him, and wanted to apologize in some way—and found myself unable to think how to do it. (Out of my sense of helplessness and wish to respond in some way, I even had a small urge to reply in kind.)

It suddenly struck me that while our culture has a universally-recognized visual gesture for anger, we don't have a gesture for apology that can be clearly recognized at a distance. In person, a sincere apology often defuses anger, while responding with anger usually escalates, sometimes even into violence. How many bad feelings—and perhaps a few freeway shootouts—could be prevented if we had a clearly-recognizable gesture for apology? Since then I have thought about gestures that could serve this function.

My first thought was of a slight bowing of the head and touching my fingers to my forehead, with the palm facing in. However, there are many situations in which this gesture wouldn't be clearly visible. We need a gesture that can be delivered out of a car window, and as easily recognized as the middle finger.

The best I've come up with so far is an extended hand, with the palm up, as if gently cradling something soft and tender. Perhaps someone can think of an even better gesture. Until then, when someone indicates they are angry at you and you can't verbally apologize, will you join me in trying out the palm-up gesture, to signify apology?

—SA

Anger is a short madness.

—Horace

127

A Species in Transition

Clearly humanity is in a period of very rapid and chaotic transition. Our ancestors, "prehumans" such as Homo Erectus, lived essentially unchanged for a million years or more in almost completely natural surroundings. The physical form of "Homo Sapiens" (us) has existed for only about 200,000 years, and the use of spoken languages may also be that old. Significant innovations in the bow and arrow occurred only about every 5,000 to 10,000 years, and agriculture and written language is less than 10,000 years old.

Compare this with the current pace that we are changing our surroundings—the discoveries and innovations reported daily in magazines and newspapers. It took some 300 years for the discovery of the germ that caused the black death, but only a few years to discover (and characterize) the AIDS virus. Recently it took only weeks to identify a previously-unknown virus that killed a number of horses and their trainer in Australia.

As little as a hundred years ago in the US, 97% of the population was directly engaged in the production of food. Now all the food we need can be produced by only 3% of the population, leaving 97% of us free to do other things than attend to survival.

Past generations dealt mostly with the challenges of raw nature, living with, and dying from, famine, disease, weather and other external causes. Now most of us live in environments that we have created for ourselves and continue to modify. Most people now die from the effects of this self-created environment—from auto accidents, chemicals, drugs, medicines, electricity, bombs, guns and other human creations. Only a lucky few die truly "natural deaths."

Centuries ago, our species was fairly well adapted to the natural world. Now we are forced to adapt to a far different, and rapidly changing, world. To take only one example, the ability to read and write, once a luxury of the educated few, has become a basic and necessary life skill.

All this puts our species in the position of traveling down an unknown winding road at successively increasing speed. One wrong turn, and our favorite experiment of nature may be "history."

In one of my favorite cartoons—from some forty years ago—an anthropologist runs excitedly out of his laboratory, shouting "Eureka! I've discovered the missing link between the anthropoidal apes and civilized human beings! It's us!"

—SA

Building Sidewalks

When a certain university was first built, all the grounds were planted with grass, without any sidewalks. After a few months, the well-worn trails clearly showed where people usually walked as they went from one building to another. Then they built sidewalks where the trails were, so that students didn't have to walk in the mud.

I have always admired the simplicity and elegance of that solution, particularly when contrasted with the usual way of doing things: elaborate and expensive planners and plans—and then the inevitable ugly fences, signs, and barriers that try to force people to walk where the planners decided that they should.

There is a general principle here that bears examining, to find out how else we could make use of its simplicity and elegance. Every culture, every subculture, and every family acts like sidewalk planners—deciding ahead of time what people *should* do, and then attempting to enforce obedience when human nature finds that the "shoulds" don't fit very well. (Lots of "shoulds" make our lives "shoulddy.")

What would it be like if instead we "planted grass" everywhere, and then noticed where people naturally liked to walk, building our social structures to accommodate our natural inclinations? There are limits to this, of course; it's appropriate to construct protective barriers at cliffs or other truly dangerous places.

If we examine a wide range of cultures, we find at least as wide a range of (often contradictory) assumptions about human nature. These assumptions are embodied in the rules, customs, and goals of each culture. The kindest thing we can say about this great variety of opinions is that they can't all be right! Any culture is the accumulated wisdom of a group of people who managed to survive somehow; after all, history is written by those who survive it. Culture also includes the accumulated stupidity of the group, as well. Growing up as a small child in Hawaii, and then moving successively to Vermont, California, Arizona, and several other places made it blazingly obvious that what one group considered important or essential was often ignored or even condemned in another. As Alfred North Whitehead said, "Learning preserves the errors of the past as well as its wisdom."

It is only in the past couple of hundred years that an increasing minority have seriously questioned their cultural assumptions about human nature, and dared to ask, "What is humanity capable of, if it is not limited by the harness and blinders of a particular culture?" I think we have only begun to discover the beauty and depth of what our humanity is capable of. Let's get on with it.

—SA

Words

It was at a party in California in the mid-1970's. Our friend Mike had arrived quite hungry, and there was a big plate of chocolate brownies on the dining-room table, so he helped himself, repeatedly. After he had eaten about nine squares, the host announced that they were marijuana brownies, and that one square would probably be enough for an adequately altered evening. Later that evening Mike was pretty far gone, especially after some time in the hot tub. As we were putting on our clothes after getting out of the hot tub, we heard Mike saying slowly out loud, "Now I'm putting on my left sock. . . . Now I'm putting on my left shoe. . . ." I laughed, and said, "Mike, we don't need a report of your activities." He replied slowly, "I know *you* don't, but *I do!*"

Even in normal states of alertness, words help us keep track of experiences by labeling them and categorizing them. We can then use these labels like a filing system, to "call up" a particular kind of experience when it's useful to us. The words on a menu bring to mind the taste and texture of the food described, to help us make a decision about what we want to order. The words are not the food; they only point to the food. This seems like a simple and obvious fact—very few people try to eat the menu—yet many people get so embroiled in the words that they never get to the food.

A word is like a handle on a suitcase; the name helps us carry a package of experiences. However, as soon as we have a name for something, there is a strong tendency to stop looking at what the name points to. Sometimes we happily carry around the suitcase without ever opening it to see what's inside. As Warren McCulloch, a pioneering neurophysiologist, used to say to his listeners, "Don't bite my finger; look where I am pointing."

—SA

Human contact is not about words. Human contact is about eye connection, about voice, about skin, about breathing. Words are something you can read in a book, you can see on a billboard, and they can be totally differentiated from human beings. Words help when people are congruent.

—Virginia Satir

Changing

Another problem with words is that while the world is always changing, words have a tendency to stand still. Take the word "breeze" or "wind." Although these words mean that air is moving, they sound as if they are something solid and unmoving that you could put in a bottle.

It really would be much clearer if we said "winding," or "breezing," or "blowing," to clearly indicate that we are pointing to a process that is continually changing.

Even something like a mountain, which we usually think of as permanent, is a slow process that might take 30 million years from beginning to end. What if we thought of it as "mountaining," to keep before us the idea of continual change? For one thing, it might keep us from getting lost when we think about "mind" as if it were a thing, like a pair of shoes. I think it was Leslie White who wrote that "Mind is minding; that's what bodies do." If we really took seriously that a noun is only a slow verb, we could transform all nouns into verbs. "I like your shirt" would become "Iing liking youring shirting." With the idea of continual change constantly surrounding us we couldn't get stuck, or blocked, or stagnant. We'd only feel ourselves slowing down, with the clear knowledge that this, too, will change.

—SA

134

Trap

Many years ago I was involved with a woman who didn't agree with some of my actions and attitudes. After considerable argument and discussion she finally concluded, "You just have a basic lack of humanity." Our relationship ended not long after this.

It wasn't until many years later that I realized how she had unintentionally trapped us both by describing our disagreement in this way. If she had said, "I don't like those attitudes and actions; I want you to change them" then I'd have a choice to comply or not, because attitudes and behaviors can be changed.

But by describing our disagreement as my "basic lack of humanity," she presupposed something about my *being* that I couldn't change, and had no choice about. Described in this way, there was no point in trying to please her, because I suffered from a "basic lack." I can change what I *do,* and how I *think* and *respond,* but I can't change who I *am.*

People get into this difficulty any time they describe someone's behavior in terms of who they *are,* instead of what they *do.* "He *is* a delinquent," "She *is* a flirt," instead of describing the behaviors that the label refers to. Besides ignoring all the other aspects of person, labeling a person's being presupposes that they can't change, and most people will accept this presupposition, just as I did.

—SA

135

What's in a Name?

When my wife, Connirae, and I decided to get married, she didn't like my last name, Stevens. I had never liked my first name, John (despite the fact that there is a room in every public building dedicated to that name), and had been known to friends as "Steve" for many years, though "Steve Stevens" always sounded a bit strange.

So I took my wife's last name, and changed my name to Steve Andreas. I had had my old name for 45 years; it seemed about time for a new one. (I would have tried to agree with her on a different name if I'd realized that I'd have to spell "Andreas" to *everyone* new on the phone, *every* time! With "Stevens" all I had to do was say "Stevens—with a 'v.'")

When I tried to change my name on my driver's license and social security, I encountered a stone wall of reverse sexism. Officials responded with blank stares, and then asked to see court papers verifying my name change—none of which would have occurred if I had been a woman who had just married.

I patiently explained to them that I can legally change my name any time I want to (and as often as I want to) without benefit of a judge, as long as I don't try to defraud anyone, and notify everyone I have business dealings with. Often I had to ask to talk to their supervisor—or their supervisor's supervisor—until I finally got grudging acquiescence.

But the real message in all this is that most people make such a fuss about names, when they're only a way to talk about and designate things. Over four hundred years ago Shakespeare wrote:

> "What's in a name? That which we call a rose
> By any other name would smell as sweet."

Despite the deaths of Romeo and Juliet—and quite a few others—most of us haven't yet gotten the message. A recent poll determined that the *main* reason (over 70%, I think) that couples decided to have another child was "to carry on the family name"—the *husband's* family name, of course! So it may be that simple sexist vanity is all it takes to overpopulate and ruin our planet.

—SA

Self-Description

Often people don't pay much attention to the words they use to describe themselves, and the consequences and ramifications of using these words. For instance, people who have had horrible experiences—particularly in early childhood—often describe themselves as "scarred for life."

In the first place, they are engaged in fortune-telling without being qualified. No one can predict the future that well. Some people continue to suffer from traumatic experiences into their later years, but many others don't.

Secondly, they don't examine the meanings of the words they use. Most people go "Oh, 'scarred for life,' Yes, terrible!" without thinking about what the words actually mean. I have quite a few scars, and none of them bother me a bit. Scar tissue is often considerably tougher than the original. Only a few scars continue to produce discomfort, and even then the discomfort is more often due to damage that never fully healed, than to the scar tissue itself. Scarring is actually a sign that the body healed itself and made itself whole again.

Another aspect of scars is that they may be visible to others, depending on where they are located. Some people who were abused as children behave as if these events were obvious and known to others. (Whether this is the reason for choosing the word "scarred" or the result of it is not clear.)

Some of my scars are still quite clear and obvious, but most of them have simply disappeared, or been incorporated into wrinkles—one of the benefits of growing older.

Even the meaning of obvious scars depends on how they are viewed. Early in this century in Germany, a visible dueling scar was considered a badge of honor. When I was in high school in New Mexico in the 1950's, many students flaunted their knife scars as a sign of bravery. Some African tribes deliberately create elaborate decorations on their skins by scarring. I have even met quite a few women with scars that made their faces much more interesting than they would have been without them.

So what does "scarred for life" really mean?—only what you choose it to mean.

—SA

A Knight in Shining Armor

Although the image is less popular now, women used to describe the ideal man as "a knight in shining armor," and quite a few men tried to live up to this image. Examine your own image of knighthood, and you can easily see how women often got what they asked for, but didn't want.

A knight in armor has a cold, hard exterior, and this makes it difficult to see the real man inside. Trapped inside that armor, he'll be unexpressive and unable to show his feelings. A knight will be up on his "high horse" a lot of the time—and he'll need help to get up there again when he falls off. He will also want to use his lance—a lot. Who's going to shine his armor and take care of his horse? Often he'll be off rescuing (other) damsels in distress, or on crusades in other lands, rather than at home with his wife and children.

The metaphors and images we use have a way of steering our thinking and our lives. It's wise to be cautious about the ones we use, and examine them to see if they are taking us where we really want to go. An old saying goes, "Be very careful what you set your heart upon, for someday it may be yours."

—SA

140

Tradition

Abraham Maslow used to delight in telling a story about an efficiency expert who was hired by the British Army during World War II to study their artillery routines, to see if they could be made more effective. The expert watched as the gun crew got into a truck and wheeled a field piece into position, and then went through the operations of loading and aiming the gun, preparing to fire. Just before firing, two of the crew walked crisply to the rear of the gun and stood at attention. After firing they went back to the gun and participated in unloading the spent casing and reloading.

When he asked the crew why the two men went to stand at attention they responded that they didn't know; that was just part of the routine they had been taught. Going up through the chain of command, asking older and older officers, he got the same puzzling answer.

Finally he asked a veteran of the Boer War to observe the routine and asked him if he knew what the two men were doing. He laughed heartily and said, "They're holding the reins of the horses so they won't run away with the gun when it fires!"

—SA

The Wisest Man in the World

A Legend of Ancient Israel
Retold by Benjamin Elkin

In days of old, so it is said, a little bee strayed into the palace of the great King Solomon. The angry servants ran to trap it. But the bee escaped from them and flew to the King for safety.

Now this King was the wisest man in the world. So wise was he that he spoke the language of every living thing: of beasts and of fowl, of creeping things and of fishes.

"Mercy, O King," pleaded the bee. "Spare me today, that I may live to serve you tomorrow."

King Solomon smiled to think that this tiny creature could ever hope to serve a mighty monarch. But he drew the curtain and gently released the bee with his own hand. "Go in peace," he said. "I require no service in return."

Through the open curtain the King saw a great caravan. There were hundreds of camels bedecked in gold.

There were apes and peacocks, and lions and tigers on jeweled leashes. And at the head of the caravan rode the proud and beautiful Queen of Sheba.

The Queen and her councilors had traveled for many weeks over the vast desert to visit the King.

King Solomon had long been expecting these visitors. He sent a group of nobles to escort them into the palace.

Dressed in his royal robes, the King seated himself upon his throne. Now this was a most wondrous throne, indeed. It was of ivory, covered with gold and precious jewels. Overhead was a golden candlestick with seven branches on each side. All around, hanging crystals flashed their rainbow colors and tinkled like heavenly harps. And most marvelous of all were the two golden lions and two golden eagles which stood on either side of the six steps leading up to the throne. For these golden lions and eagles would permit no one to lie to the King. If anyone dared to tell an untruth, the lions would roar and the eagles would scream.

When the Queen of Sheba entered she could not hide her surprise at King Solomon's splendor. "May the King live forever," she said. "I come to offer you the true friendship of my country."

At once, the golden lions roared and the eagles screamed. For the Queen of Sheba spoke falsely; she had not come as a true friend. But knowing naught of these lions and eagles, the Queen graciously bowed. To her ears, this was another royal salute. In truth, she had long been jealous of King Solomon's fame. And in this visit she hoped to shame him before his own people and before the whole world.

During the next few days the Queen of Sheba did her best to prove that her host was not really wise. She tested his wisdom with difficult riddles. But all of them he readily answered.

Once the Queen brought to him a large diamond which had a curved, twisting hole. "Is it within your power to draw a thread through a winding hole?" she asked.

King Solomon only smiled and sent for a silkworm. The worm crawled through the hole, drawing a thread of silk right through it.

Another time, the Queen sent in sixty little boys and girls, all dressed alike. "If it please Your Majesty," she said, "tell me from your throne which are the boys and which the girls."

To his servants King Solomon said, "Place a basin of water before each of the children and bid them wash their faces."

Then the boys splashed water on their faces while the girls daintily dabbed the water with their fingertips. And so the King could easily tell them apart.

Once the King and Queen saw that a little dog had fallen into a deep pool. The water was so low that the dog could not be reached. King Solomon tossed a branch into the water for the dog to cling to.

"I would not have done so," said the Queen. "It is better to drown speedily than to starve slowly." And she and her councilors were happy that the King had at last done something so unwise.

But King Solomon did not stop to reply. He showed his men how to block the nearby stream with rocks. As the stream overflowed into the pool, the water rose higher and higher. Soon the branch floated up within reach, and the dog was safely lifted out.

That night the Queen of Sheba met with her councilors. "Thus far we have had no success," she said, "and tomorrow will be our final chance. The King has invited guests from many lands to a banquet in my honor. For this banquet we must find a trick which will show them that King Solomon is not wise, but a fool."

"Such a trick have we found, Your Majesty," said the councilors.

From King Solomon's garden the councilors plucked a flower. They ordered their craftsmen to make ninety-nine false flowers exactly like it. And then they placed just one fresh flower among the ninety-nine false ones. The copies were so perfect that the Queen of Sheba herself could not point out the real one.

"Well done," said the Queen. "King Solomon will surely pick a false flower as coming fresh from his own garden. By tonight he will be a joke among all the nations."

A gardener heard this and reported it to the King.

But King Solomon had become so proud and confident that he refused to be concerned. "It matters not," he said. "It suits me well that they should prove my wisdom before the multitude, and I fear not what they may do."

That night the palace gleamed with light as hundreds of guests came to honor King Solomon and the Queen of Sheba.

At just the right moment the Queen said, "Your gracious Majesty. Our craftsmen beg that you judge their work. Among these flowers only one comes from your garden. The others have been created by my servants in your honor. Won't you select your own flower and let my servants know how theirs compare?"

At first the King was confident of his ability to choose. But when he sniffed the flowers they were all equally fragrant. He felt them, and they were all petal smooth. In beautiful color and appearance, they were identical.

Perhaps this was a trick, and *all* the flowers were false. Then he would be wrong no matter which one he selected.

Never had King Solomon believed that he could thus be entrapped before the guests. As he stood there, puzzled, the guests began to whisper. What was wrong? Couldn't the King even pick out his own flower from his own garden? Perhaps he was not so wise after all! Even the loyal servants became nervous. Why did not the King make his choice and stop this foolish whispering among the guests?

Then King Solomon felt something tickle his hand. A little bee had landed there. "I am at your service, Your Majesty," whispered the bee. It circled low over the flowers. Then it crawled into the one flower which had honey inside.

No one else had seen the little bee. King Solomon leaned over and plucked out the one flower with the bee in it; the one flower which had grown in his garden.

"Yes," said the King, "your craftsmen are indeed skilled. I have been admiring their work. But the false cannot be true. The others are false, and this one is true."

The Queen checked for the craftsmen's secret mark and then bowed low. Truly, this was the single genuine flower. As the audience applauded, the Queen was finally convinced.

The very next day, the Queen of Sheba and her councilors signed a treaty of friendship with King Solomon.

They left for home, bearing many rich gifts.

Later, in the quiet of his rooms, King Solomon thought gratefully of the little bee which had served him so well. He humbly bowed his head. "I have been too proud," he thought. "None is so great that he needs no help, and none is so small that he cannot give it."

Surely, wisdom is given
to all living things,
And the tiniest creatures
are teachers of kings.

Dreaming

I once was with somebody I liked very much—an older person, when I was considerably younger than I am now. That person said, "Spend at least fifteen minutes a day weaving dreams. And if you weave a hundred, at least two of them will have a life." So continue with a dream and don't worry whether it can happen or not; weave it first. Many people have killed their dreams by figuring out whether they could do them or not before they dream them. So, if you've a first-rate dreamer, dream it out—several of them—and then see what realities can come to make them happen, instead of saying, "Oh, my God. With this reality, what can I dream?"

—Virginia Satir

Nothing happens unless first a dream.

 —Carl Sandburg

All people dream, but not all equally. Those who dream by night in the dusty recesses of their minds wake in the day to find it was vanity; but the dreamers of the day are dangerous, for they may act their dreams with open eyes, to make it possible.

—Lawrence of Arabia

Patience

There is here no measuring with time, no year matters, and ten years are nothing. Being an artist means, not reckoning and counting, but ripening like the tree which does not force its sap and stands confident in the storms of spring without the fear that after them may come no summer. It does come. But it comes only to the patient, who are there as though eternity lay before them, so unconcernedly still and wide. I learn it daily, learn it with pain to which I am grateful: *patience* is everything!

—Rainer Maria Rilke

Reprinted from LETTERS TO A YOUNG POET by Rainer Maria Rilke, translated from the German by M. D. Herter Norton, with the permission of W. W. Norton & Co., Inc. Copyright 1934 by W. W. Norton & Company, Inc., renewed 1962 by M. D. Herter Norton. Revised edition copyright 1954 by W. W. Norton & Company, Inc.

Life is too short to be hurried.

—SA

Hope

Hope is a good breakfast, but it is a bad supper.

—Francis Bacon

Never deprive someone of hope; it might be all they have.

—H. Jackson Brown, Jr.

You can count the seeds in an apple,
but you can't count the apples in a seed.

(SU)

Albert Szent-gyorgi, who got a Nobel prize for discovering Vitamin C, once described how he liked to fish—which was a metaphor for how he lived his life. "When I go fishing, I always use an enormous hook. People often ask me why I use such a big hook. I explain to them that I know I'm not going to catch a fish anyway, and it is much more exciting to not catch a big fish than to not catch a little fish."

—SA

Hope for everything.
Expect nothing.

—SA

Hope is itself a species of happiness, and, perhaps, the chief happiness which this world affords.

—Samuel Johnson

Near Miss

My youngest son, Darian, bears a half-inch scar high on his left cheek, less than an inch from his eye. It happened when he was about 18 months old. I was carrying him in a backpack while hiking, and bent down to go under some overhanging branches. I didn't bend down quite low enough to clear them, and a sharp branch gave him a severe gouge. I felt bad enough about hurting him; I have often thought how bad I'd feel if I had walked just an inch to the left, and the stick had ruined his eye instead of just gouging his cheek. I was lucky, just as when I have drifted over the highway center line briefly but there were no oncoming cars—or all those other little mistakes we all make every day that have no significant consequences. Often when someone harms someone else it's mostly because of being unlucky—making one of those little everyday mistakes at the wrong time or place.

Then there are also the responses of the other people involved. Perhaps that sharp tree branch *was* headed directly toward Darian's eye, and he moved his head to avoid it. Or perhaps not. But surely sometimes it takes more than one person's mistake to create a tragedy.

—SA

Fortune

A farmer lived in a very poor and remote village in China. He was considered quite well-to-do, because he owned a horse which he used for plowing and for transportation. One day his horse ran away and could not be found. All his neighbors exclaimed how terrible this was, but the farmer simply said, "Maybe."

A few days later the horse returned, bringing two wild horses with it. His neighbors all rejoiced at his good fortune, but the farmer just said, "Maybe."

The next day the farmer's son tried to ride one of the wild horses, but the horse threw him and broke his leg. The neighbors all offered their sympathy for his misfortune, but the farmer again just said, "Maybe."

The next week conscription officers came to the village to take young men for the army. They couldn't take the farmer's son because of his broken leg. When the neighbors told him how lucky he was, the farmer replied "Maybe." . . .

—SA (with thanks to Al Huang)

Luck

Driving on a narrow curving mountain road in a heavy spring California rain, rounding a bend, there it was: a large fir tree—two-and-a-half feet in diameter—lying across the road, branches still swaying, the remaining roots still popping with the strain of the fallen trunk.

My first thought was of the inconvenience. I'd have to backtrack fifteen miles to take another road, and that would make me a half-hour late for my meeting.

But as I drove back down the road I had other thoughts. If I had arrived perhaps ten seconds earlier, the tree would have fallen right across my car, and I wouldn't have been concerned about being a little late for a meeting! If I had driven even a tiny bit faster, I'd have been ten seconds earlier.

How many times in my life have I escaped death by an eyelash like this? I know of several. How many other narrow escapes did I not even recognize? How often did I miss death by being a minute or two early or late on my way to the grocery store, or by taking one road rather than other? Thinking of this makes me feel lucky to have lived so long.

Ten years ago, when my mother died, I sent out a letter to her friends. In it I explored this theme, using events she had told me about during her lifetime.

She died not. . .

. . . at birth in 1902 in New York
    weighing less than a drawn frying chicken
    thrust into a less-than-sanitary world
    innocent of incubators.

. . . at eighteen on a curving road
    her companion veering to safety
    on a gravel pile (who put it there?)
    to avoid the speeding oncoming car.

. . . on a sailboat in Bermuda
    knocked down by her attacker
    horizon replaced by swirling storm clouds
    released, as he frantically took the boat to harbor.

. . . in the attack on Hawaii in 1941
    saved by the stupidity of the Japanese Admirals
    who underestimated the stupidity of the American
        Admirals
    and who decided not to invade
    (later it was said that they could have
    captured the islands with a thousand men).

. . . caught in an unknown undertow
    exhausted, with a last desperate effort
    pushing her 6-year-old son (myself) toward shore
    sinking under, her toes touching sand
    and hope, and the energy for a few more strokes.

. . . of "chronic rheumatic fever" in the 1950's
a "non-existent" disease at the time
for which there was no known treatment,
experimenting with her doctor
and exploring her own mind
in the bedridden hours that stretched into years.

. . . at the hands of one of the FBI's "ten most wanted men"
who knocked at her door in Albuquerque
asked to make some phone calls
and stayed awhile.

. . . of a stroke in the late seventies (hers, too)
that weakened her right side
robbed her of her treasured fluency with words
casting a shadow of caution over her days.

. . . of how many other
not-quite-synchronous events or non-events
that barely missed her in passing
unnoticed and unacknowledged?

. . . like an old juniper tree
in the southwestern desert she loved so much
twisted by the wind and heat
shaped by storms and browsing animals
trunk split and burnt
yet with green branches still reaching for the sun.

. . . leaving her 83-year-old body behind her
three days after Christmas 1985
laying down a burden
grown heavy with time.

. . . In the hearts and minds of those who knew her
writing out of her struggle to understand life
always doing her best, like all of us
and like all of us, sometimes finding that none
   too good,
a sign to move on and try again, . . . and again. . . . . .

—SA (1985)

Ledger of Life

Faith is the seed,
Patience the plow,
Love is the planter;
The season is Now.

Drouth in the summer,
Flood in the fall;
Hope is the credit
Extended to all.

—Robert Lee Brothers

From *Robert Lee Brothers: The Collected Poems* edited by Susan Ford Wiltshire, Ph.D. (in preparation).

The Man Who Planted Trees
By Jean Giono

For a human character to reveal truly exceptional qual-
ities, one must have the good fortune to be able to observe
its performance over many years. If this performance is de-
void of all egoism, if its guiding motive is unparalleled
generosity, if it is absolutely certain that there is no
thought of recompense and that, in addition, it has left its
visible mark upon the earth, then there can be no mistake.

About forty years ago I was taking a long trip on foot
over mountain heights quite unknown to tourists, in that
ancient region where the Alps thrust down into Provence.
All this, at the time I embarked upon my long walk
through these deserted regions, was barren and colorless
land. Nothing grew there but wild lavender.

I was crossing the area at its widest point, and after
three days' walking, found myself in the midst of unparalleled desolation. I camped near the vestiges of an abandoned village. I had run out of water the day before, and

The Man Who Planted Trees by Jean Giono, reprinted with permission from
Chelsea Green Publishing Company, Vermont. Chelsea Green has published an
illustrated edition, with wood engravings by Michael McCurdy. To order or for
a free catalog, call 1 (800) 639-4099.

had to find some. These clustered houses, although in ruins, like an old wasps' nest, suggested that there must once have been a spring or well here. There was indeed a spring, but it was dry. The five or six houses, roofless, gnawed by wind and rain, the tiny chapel with its crumbling steeple, stood about like the houses and chapels in living villages, but all life had vanished.

It was a fine June day, brilliant with sunlight, but over this unsheltered land, high in the sky, the wind blew with unendurable ferocity. It growled over the carcasses of the houses like a lion disturbed at its meal. I had to move my camp.

After five hours' walking I had still not found water and there was nothing to give me any hope of finding any. All about me was the same dryness, the same coarse grasses. I thought I glimpsed in the distance a small black silhouette, upright, and took it for the trunk of a solitary tree. In any case I started toward it. It was a shepherd. Thirty sheep were lying about him on the baking earth.

He gave me a drink from his water-gourd and, a little later, took me to his cottage in a fold of the plain. He drew his water—excellent water—from a very deep natural well above which he had constructed a primitive winch.

The man spoke little. This is the way of those who live alone, but one felt that he was sure of himself, and confident in his assurance. That was unexpected in this barren country. He lived, not in a cabin, but in a real house built of stone that bore plain evidence of how his own efforts had reclaimed the ruin he had found there on his arrival. His roof was strong and sound. The wind on its tiles made the sound of the sea upon its shore.

The place was in order, the dishes washed, the floor swept, his rifle oiled; his soup was boiling over the fire. I noticed then that he was cleanly shaved, that all his buttons were firmly sewed on, that his clothing had been mended with the meticulous care that makes the mending invisible. He shared his soup with me and afterwards, when I offered my tobacco pouch, he told me that he did not smoke. His dog, as silent as himself, was friendly without being servile.

It was understood from the first that I should spend the night there; the nearest village was still more than a day and a half away. And besides I was perfectly familiar with the nature of the rare villages in that region. There were four or five of them scattered well apart from each other on these mountain slopes, among white oak thickets, at the extreme end of the wagon roads. They were inhabited by charcoal burners, and the living was bad. Families, crowded together in a climate that is excessively harsh both in winter and in summer, found no escape from the unceasing conflict of personalities. Irrational ambition reached inordinate proportions in the continual desire for escape. The men took their wagonloads of charcoal to the town, then returned. The soundest characters broke under the perpetual grind. The women nursed their grievances. There was rivalry in everything, over the price of charcoal as over a pew in the church, over warring virtues as over warring vices as well as over the ceaseless combat between virtue and vice. And over all there was the wind, also ceaseless, to rasp upon the nerves. There were epidemics of suicide and frequent cases of insanity, usually homicidal.

The shepherd went to fetch a small sack and poured out a heap of acorns on the table. He began to inspect them, one by one, with great concentration, separating the good from the bad. I smoked my pipe. I did offer to help him. He told me that it was his job. And in fact, seeing the care he devoted to the task, I did not insist. That was the whole of our conversation. When he had set aside a large enough pile of good acorns he counted them out by tens, meanwhile eliminating the small ones or those which were slightly cracked, for now he examined them more closely. When he had thus selected one hundred perfect acorns he stopped and we went to bed.

There was peace in being with this man. The next day I asked if I might rest here for a day. He found it quite natural—or, to be more exact, he gave me the impression that nothing could startle him. The rest was not absolutely necessary, but I was interested and wished to know more about him. He opened the pen and led his flock to pasture. Before leaving, he plunged his sack of carefully selected and counted acorns into a pail of water.

I noticed that he carried for a stick an iron rod as thick as my thumb and about a yard and a half long. Resting myself by walking, I followed a path parallel to his. His pasture was in a valley. He left the dog in charge of the little flock and climbed toward where I stood. I was afraid that he was about to rebuke me for my indiscretion, but it was not that at all: this was the way he was going, and he invited me to go along if I had nothing better to do. He climbed to the top of the ridge, about a hundred yards away.

There he began thrusting his iron rod into the earth, making a hole in which he planted an acorn; then he refilled the hole. He was planting oak trees. I asked him if the land belonged to him. He answered no. Did he know whose it was? He did not. He supposed it was community property, or perhaps belonged to people who cared nothing about it. He was not interested in finding out whose it was. He planted his hundred acorns with the greatest care.

After the midday meal he resumed his planting. I suppose I must have been fairly insistent in my questioning, for he answered me. For three years he had been planting trees in this wilderness. He had planted one hundred thousand. Of the hundred thousand, twenty thousand had sprouted. Of the twenty thousand he still expected to lose about half, to rodents or to the unpredictable designs of Providence. There remained ten thousand oak trees to grow where nothing had grown before.

That was when I began to wonder about the age of this man. He was obviously over fifty. Fifty-five, he told me. His name was Elzéard Bouffier. He had once had a farm in the lowlands. There he had had his life. He had lost his only son, then his wife. He had withdrawn into this solitude where his pleasure was to live leisurely with his lambs and his dog. It was his opinion that this land was dying for want of trees. He added that, having no very pressing business of his own, he had resolved to remedy this state of affairs.

Since I was at that time, in spite of my youth, leading a solitary life, I understood how to deal gently with solitary spirits. But my very youth forced me to consider the future in relation to myself and to a certain quest for happiness. I told him that in thirty years his ten thousand oaks would be magnificent. He answered quite simply that if God granted him life, in thirty years he would have planted so many more that these ten thousand would be like a drop of water in the ocean.

Besides, he was now studying the reproduction of beech trees and had a nursery of seedlings grown from beechnuts near his cottage. The seedlings, which he had protected from his sheep with a wire fence, were very beautiful. He was also considering birches for the valleys where, he told me, there was a certain amount of moisture a few yards below the surface of the soil.

The next day we parted.

The following year came the War of 1914, in which I was involved for the next five years. An infantryman hardly had time for reflecting upon trees. To tell the truth, the thing itself had made no impression upon me; I had considered it as a hobby, a stamp collection, and forgotten it.

The war over, I found myself possessed of a tiny demobilization bonus and a huge desire to breathe fresh air for a while. It was with no other objective that I again took the road to the barren lands.

The countryside had not changed. However, beyond the deserted village I glimpsed in the distance a sort of greyish mist that covered the mountaintops like a carpet. Since the day before, I had begun to think again of the shepherd tree-planter. "Ten thousand oaks," I reflected, "really take up quite a bit of space."

I had seen too many men die during those five years not to imagine easily that Elzéard Bouffier was dead, especially since, at twenty, one regards men of fifty as old men with nothing left to do but die. He was not dead. As a matter of fact, he was extremely spry. He had changed jobs. Now he had only four sheep but, instead, a hundred beehives. He had got rid of the sheep because they threatened his young trees. For, he told me (and I saw for myself), the war had disturbed him not at all. He had imperturbably continued to plant.

The oaks of 1910 were then ten years old and taller than either of us. It was an impressive spectacle. I was literally speechless and, as he did not talk, we spent the whole day walking in silence through his forest. In three sections, it measured eleven kilometers in length and three kilometers at its greatest width. When you remembered that all this had sprung from the hands and the soul of this one man, without technical resources, you understood that men could be as effectual as God in other realms than that of destruction.

He had pursued his plan, and beech trees as high as my shoulder, spreading out as far as the eye could reach, confirmed it. He showed me handsome clumps of birch planted five years before—that is, in 1915, when I had been fighting at Verdun. He had set them out in all the valleys where he had guessed—and rightly—that there was moisture almost at the surface of the ground. They were as delicate as young girls, and very well established.

Creation seemed to come about in a sort of chain reaction. He did not worry about it; he was determinedly pursuing his task in all its simplicity; but as we went back toward the village I saw water flowing in brooks that had been dry since the memory of man. This was the most impressive result of chain reaction that I had seen. These dry streams had once, long ago, run with water. Some of the dreary villages I mentioned before had been built on the sites of ancient Roman settlements, traces of which still remained; and archaeologists, exploring there, had found fishhooks where, in the twentieth century, cisterns were needed to assure a small supply of water.

The wind, too, scattered seeds. As the water reappeared, so there reappeared willows, rushes, meadows, gardens, flowers, and a certain purpose in being alive. But the transformation took place so gradually that it became part of the pattern without causing any astonishment. Hunters, climbing into the wilderness in pursuit of hares or wild boar, had of course noticed the sudden growth of little trees, but had attributed it to some natural caprice of the earth. That is why no one meddled with Elzéard Bouffier's work. If he had been detected he would have had opposition. He was indetectable. Who in the villages or in the administration could have dreamed of such perseverance in a magnificent generosity?

To have anything like a precise idea of this exceptional character one must not forget that he worked in total solitude: so total that, toward the end of his life, he lost the habit of speech. Or perhaps it was that he saw no need for it.

In 1933 he received a visit from a forest ranger who notified him of an order against lighting fires out of doors for fear of endangering the growth of this *natural* forest. It was the first time, the man told him naively, that he had ever heard of a forest growing of its own accord. At that time Bouffier was about to plant beeches at a spot some twelve kilometers from his cottage. In order to avoid travelling back and forth—for he was then seventy-five—he planned to build a stone cabin right at the plantation. The next year he did so.

In 1935 a whole delegation came from the Government to examine the "natural forest." There was a high official from the Forest Service, a deputy, technicians. There was a great deal of ineffectual talk. It was decided that something must be done and, fortunately, nothing was done except the only helpful thing: the whole forest was placed under the protection of the State, and charcoal burning prohibited. For it was impossible not to be captivated by the beauty of those young trees in the fullness of health, and they cast their spell over the deputy himself.

A friend of mine was among the forestry officers of the delegation. To him I explained the mystery. One day the following week we went together to see Elzéard Bouffier. We found him hard at work, some ten kilometers from the spot where the inspection had taken place.

This forester was not my friend for nothing. He was aware of values. He knew how to keep silent. I delivered the eggs I had brought as a present. We shared our lunch among the three of us and spent several hours in wordless contemplation of the countryside.

165

In the direction from which we had come the slopes were covered with trees twenty to twenty-five feet tall. I remembered how the land had looked in 1913: a desert. . . . Peaceful, regular toil, the vigorous mountain air, frugality and, above all, serenity of spirit had endowed this old man with awe-inspiring health. He was one of God's athletes. I wondered how many more acres he was going to cover with trees.

Before leaving, my friend simply made a brief suggestion about certain species of trees that the soil here seemed particularly suited for. He did not force the point. "For the very good reason," he told me later, "that Bouffier knows more about it than I do." At the end of an hour's walking—having turned it over in his mind—he added, "He knows a lot more about it than anybody. He's discovered a wonderful way to be happy!"

It was thanks to this officer that not only the forest but also the happiness of the man was protected. He delegated three rangers to the task, and so terrorized them that they remained proof against all the bottles of wine the charcoal burners could offer.

The only serious danger to the work occurred during the war of 1939. As cars were being run on gazogenes (wood-burning generators), there was never enough wood. Cutting was started among the oaks of 1910, but the area was so far from any railroads that the enterprise turned out to be financially unsound. It was abandoned. The shepherd had seen nothing of it. He was thirty kilometers away, peacefully continuing his work, ignoring the war of '39 as he had ignored that of '14.

I saw Elzéard Bouffier for the last time in June of 1945. He was then eighty-seven. I had started back along the route through the wastelands; but now, in spite of the disorder in which the war had left the country, there was a bus running between the Durance Valley and the mountain. I attributed the fact that I no longer recognized the scenes of my earlier journeys to this relatively speedy transportation. It seemed to me, too, that the route took me through new territory. It took the name of a village to convince me that I was actually in that region that had been all ruins and desolation.

The bus put me down at Vergons. In 1913 this hamlet of ten or twelve houses had three inhabitants. They had been savage creatures, hating one another, living by trapping game, little removed, both physically and morally, from the conditions of prehistoric man. All about them nettles were feeding upon the remains of abandoned houses. Their condition had been beyond hope. For them, nothing but to await death—a situation which rarely predisposes to virtue.

Everything was changed. Even the air. Instead of the harsh dry winds that used to attack me, a gentle breeze was blowing, laden with scents. A sound like water came from the mountains: it was the wind in the forest. Most amazing of all, I heard the actual sound of water falling into a pool. I saw that a fountain had been built, that it flowed freely and—what touched me most—that someone had planted a linden beside it, a linden that must have been four years old, already in full leaf, the incontestable symbol of resurrection.

Besides, Vergons bore evidence of labor at the sort of undertaking for which hope is required. Hope, then, had returned. Ruins had been cleared away, dilapidated walls torn down and five houses restored. Now there were twenty-eight inhabitants, four of them young married couples. The new houses, freshly plastered, were surrounded by gardens where vegetables and flowers grew in orderly confusion, cabbages and roses, leeks and snapdragons, celery and anemones. It was now a village where one would like to live.

From that point on I went on foot. The war just finished had not yet allowed the full blooming of life, but Lazarus was out of the tomb. On the lower slopes of the mountain I saw little fields of barley and of rye; deep in the narrow valleys the meadows were turning green.

It has taken only eight years since then for the whole countryside to glow with health and prosperity. On the site of ruins I had seen in 1913 now stand neat farms, cleanly plastered, testifying to a happy and comfortable life. The old streams, fed by the rains and snows that the forest conserves, are flowing again. Their waters have been channeled. On each farm, in groves of maples, fountain pools overflow onto carpets of fresh mint. Little by little the villages have been rebuilt. People from the plains, where land is costly, have settled here, bringing youth, motion, the spirit of adventure. Along the roads you meet hearty men and women, boys and girls who understand laughter and have recovered a taste for picnics. Counting the former population, unrecognizable now that they live in comfort, more than ten thousand people owe their happiness to Elzéard Bouffier.

When I reflect that one man, armed only with his own physical and moral resources, was able to cause this land of Canaan to spring from the wasteland, I am convinced that in spite of everything, humanity is admirable. But when I compute the unfailing greatness of spirit and the tenacity of benevolence that it must have taken to achieve this result, I am taken with an immense respect for that old and unlearned peasant who was able to complete a work worthy of God.

Elzéard Bouffier died peacefully in 1947 at the hospice in Banon.

The Man Who Planted Trees is a work of fiction. Yet the principles are true, and it is these truths that give this story its vitality. In that sense, it is a true story. The original title of this story was "The man who planted hope and grew happiness."

Success

To laugh often and much; to win the respect of intelligent people and the affection of children; to earn the appreciation of honest critics and endure the betrayal of false friends; to appreciate beauty, to find the best in others; to leave the world a bit better, whether by a healthy child, a garden patch or a redeemed social condition; to know that even one life has breathed easier because you have lived. This is to have succeeded.

—Ralph Waldo Emerson

I am only one,
But still I am one.
I cannot do everything,
But still I can do something;
And because I cannot do everything
I will not refuse to do the something that I can do.

—Edward Everett Hale

Ritual

At Caltech, where I was an undergraduate over forty years ago, an interesting tradition was observed during every morning of final exam week. Legend had it that in previous years some students had slept late and missed their scheduled finals. In order to make sure this didn't happen in the future, it was decided that every student in the dorms who had a way of producing sound—mostly record players in those days—would play Richard Wagner's "The Ride of the Valkyries" at top volume. This is not a timid piece of music; it is a triumphal and exhilarating celebration of the ascension into heaven of Norse heroes who had died valiantly in battle. The Valkyries were the maidens of Odin who conducted the souls of heroes slain in battle to Valhalla. The experience of standing in an open courtyard and being bathed in this music from some twenty different sources at full volume—and all out-of-sync—is impossible to describe.

Experiencing all this while contemplating the finals to come, and the knowledge that it was too late to do any more preparation, put me in a state of "go for it" and "do or die" that served me well during the exams. After four years of this, the two experiences were welded together in my mind. Ever since, whenever I'm faced with a challenge and I need that exhilarated state of readiness, the Ride of the Valkyries begins to play in my mind—from multiple sources, at high volume, and out-of-sync.

—SA

A Small World

My friend David was giving a presentation to several hundred people at a major psychotherapy conference. After the applause, he was talking with several people who had questions. Since I hadn't seen David in some time, I waited to have a brief visit with him. After most of the people had walked away, David turned to me and said, "Steve, I'd like to introduce you to my father."

I was stunned, and had difficulty functioning for a few seconds. Why? Because I put myself in David's place, and I had *never thought* of my father being in the audience when I make a presentation. It's not that I had thought about how nice it would be to have my father in the audience and then dismissed it because my father died when I was nine years old. *The possibility simply never entered my mind until that moment.* And when it did, it was like a thunderclap that split open my tiny world.

I loved the idea; I would like my father to witness my small successes in life. Since that day my father is always present in the group—unobtrusive, two-thirds of the way back, on the left side—sometimes smiling, sometimes thoughtful, sometimes shaking his head, or nodding in agreement—but always there.

—SA

171

The Silken Tent

She is as in a field a silken tent
At midday when a sunny summer breeze
Has dried the dew and all its ropes relent,
So that in guys it gently sways at ease,
And its supporting central cedar pole,
That is its pinnacle to heavenward
And signifies the sureness of the soul,
Seems to owe naught to any single cord,
But strictly held by none, is loosely bound
By countless silken ties of love and thought
To everything on earth the compass round,
And only by one's going slightly taut
In the capriciousness of summer air
Is of the slightest bondage made aware.

—Robert Frost

Easter 1956

The springing grass and flowering peach
Have chosen colors from the sun
To blaze with life and being; each
With its soft brilliance sweeps the air

A sequin brightens in the sun
But cannot choose a hue to wear
And so it scatters every one
Across a cheek I cannot reach

I watch the brilliance dancing there
With thoughts too swift and light for speech
Her being I can only share
Through colors borrowed from the sun

—SA

The Sound of a Butterfly's Wings

As if a lone dove flew to rest in evening
And this morning I heard the faintest echo of its passing
In soft sunlight
    Unexpectedly
        Impossibly!
Upon my ear
Upon the air
The gentle clasp of a butterfly's wings

          —SA (1966)

Vuja De

"Deja vu" literally means "I have seen this before"—
that eerie feeling you get when it seems as if a part of your
life is happening all over again, exactly as it did before.

A friend of mine pointed out that "vuja de" could be
used to name the sudden realization that you're doing
something for the first time!

    —SA

Lightness in Living

The intelligent man finds almost everything ridiculous, the sensible man hardly anything.

 —Goethe

Only the insane take themselves seriously.

—Max Beerbohm

You're only here for a short while, so have a few laughs and don't take things so seriously—especially yourself.

 —Mark Twain

Angels can fly because they take themselves lightly.

—G. K. Chesterton

The Moving Finger writes;
    and having writ,
Moves on: nor all thy
    Piety nor Wit
Shall lure it back to cancel
    half a Line,
Nor all thy Tears wash out
    a Word of it.

—Omar Khayyám

From *The Rubáiyát* (Edward Fitzgerald) #71.

Ah Love! could thou and I
    with Fate conspire
To grasp this sorry Scheme
    of Things entire,
Would not we shatter it to
    bits—and then
Re-mould it nearer to the
    Heart's Desire!

—Omar Khayyám

From *The Rubáiyát* (Edward Fitzgerald) #99.

Rise up, why mourn this transient world of men?
Pass your whole life in gratitude and joy.
Had humankind been freed from womb and tomb,
When would your time have come to live and love?

—Omar Khayaam

There are no adults.
All of us are children.
Some of us are children
      pretending to be adults,
Some of us are pretending very badly,
And some of us have forgotten
      that we are children
      pretending to be adults.

—SA

Life is a flame
That is always burning itself out,
But it catches fire again
Every time a child is born.

—George Bernard Shaw

Life

Life is a play! 'Tis not its length, but its performance that counts.

—Seneca

We are all in the gutter, but some of us are looking at the stars.

—Oscar Wilde

Live your life
As an exclamation!
Not an explanation.

—H. Jackson Brown, Jr.

Wild Strawberry

A man traveling across a field encountered a tiger. He fled, the tiger after him. Coming to a precipice, he caught hold of the root of a wild vine and swung himself down over the edge. The tiger sniffed at him from above. Trembling, the man looked down to where, far below, another tiger was waiting to eat him. Only the vine sustained him.

Two mice, one white and one black, little by little started to gnaw away the vine. The man saw a luscious strawberry near him. Grasping the vine with one hand, he plucked the strawberry with the other. How sweet it tasted!

—Paul Reps

From *Zen Flesh, Zen Bones: A collection of Zen and pre-Zen writings,* compiled by Paul Reps. © 1957 Charles E. Tuttle Company, Inc.

Now

It is only this,
no draft nor final manuscript
survives with which to speculate,
for I have burned them.
No edition has a date,
I distinguish no printings,
number and sign no copies
so what you hold, collector,
will not appreciate.
Do not put this on your shelf, critic,
for the special paper dissolves in air.
Read, that is all;
now is the only time
to take the wafer of our sacrament
before it vanishes
This is all there is.

—Peter Goblen

From *Journey Through the Light,* p.5. © 1973, Peter Goblen, Koheleth Publishing Co., San Francisco CA.

Three Questions
by Leo Tolstoy

It once occurred to a certain king, that if he always knew the right time to begin everything; if he knew who were the right people to listen to and whom to avoid; and, above all, if he always knew what was the most important thing to do, he would never fail in anything he might undertake.

And this thought having occurred to him, he had it proclaimed throughout his kingdom that he would give a great reward to anyone who would teach him what was the right time for every action, and who were the most necessary people, and how he might know what was the most important thing to do.

And learned men came to the King, but they all answered his questions differently.

In reply to the first question, some said that to know the right time for every action one must draw up in advance a table of days, months, and years, and must live

From SHORT STORIES OF LEO TOLSTOY, VOLUME 2 by Leo Tolstoy, translated by Rosalind A. Zoglin. Copyright © 1966 and renewed 1994 by Random House, Inc. Reprinted by permission of Random House, Inc.

strictly according to it. Only thus, said they, could everything be done at its proper time. Others declared that it was impossible to decide beforehand the right time for every action; but that, not letting oneself be absorbed in idle pastimes, one should always attend to all that was going on and then do what was most needful. Others, again, said that however attentive the King might be to what was going on, it was impossible for one man to decide correctly the right time for every action, but that he should have a council of wise men who would help him to fix the proper time for everything.

But then again others said there were some things which could not wait to be laid before a council, but about which one had at once to decide whether to undertake them or not. But in order to decide that, one must know beforehand what was going to happen. It is only magicians who know that; and, therefore, in order to know the right time for every action, one must consult magicians.

Equally various were the answers to the second question. Some said, the people the King most needed were his councilors; others, the priests; others, the doctors; while some said the warriors were the most necessary.

To the third question, as to what was the most important occupation: some replied that the most important thing in the world was science. Others said it was skill in warfare; and others, again, that it was religious worship.

All the answers being different, the King agreed with none of them, and gave the reward to none. But still wishing to find the right answers to his questions, he decided to consult a hermit widely renowned for his wisdom.

The hermit lived in a wood which he never quitted, and he received none but common folk. So the King put on simple clothes, and before reaching the hermit's cell dismounted from his horse, and, leaving his bodyguard behind, went on alone.

When the King approached, the hermit was digging the ground in front of his hut. Seeing the King, he greeted him and went on digging. The hermit was frail and weak, and each time he stuck his spade into the ground and turned a little earth, he breathed heavily.

The King went up to him and said: "I have come to you, wise hermit, to ask you to answer three questions: How can I learn to do the right thing at the right time? Who are the people I most need, and to whom should I, therefore, pay more attention than to the rest? And, what affairs are the most important, and need my first attention?"

The hermit listened to the King, but answered nothing. He just spat on his hand and recommenced digging.

"You are tired," said the King, "Let me take the spade and work awhile for you."

"Thanks!" said the hermit, and, giving the spade to the King, he sat down on the ground.

When he had dug two beds, the King stopped and repeated his questions. The hermit again gave no answer, but rose, stretched out his hand for the spade and said:

"Now rest awhile—and let me work a bit."

But the King did not give him the spade, and continued to dig. One hour passed, and another. The sun began to sink behind the trees, and the King at last stuck the spade into the ground, and said:

"I came to you, wise man, for an answer to my questions. If you can give me none, tell me so I will return home."

"Here comes someone running," said the hermit, "Let us see who it is."

The King turned round, and saw a bearded man come running out of the wood. The man held his hands pressed against his stomach, and blood was flowing from under them. When he reached the King, he fell fainting on the ground, moaning feebly. The King and the hermit unfastened the man's clothing. There was a large wound in his stomach. The King washed it as best he could, and bandaged it with his handkerchief and with a towel the hermit had. But the blood would not stop flowing, and the King again and again removed the bandage soaked with warm blood, and washed and rebandaged the wound. When at last the blood ceased flowing, the man revived and asked for something to drink. The King brought fresh water and gave it to him. Meanwhile the sun had set, and it had become cool. So the King, with the hermit's help, carried the wounded man into the hut and laid him on the bed. Lying on the bed the man closed his eyes and was quiet; but the King was so tired with his walk and with the work he had done, that he crouched down on the threshold, and also fell asleep—so soundly that he slept all through the short summer night. When he awoke in the morning, it was long before he could remember where he was or who was the strange bearded man lying on the bed and gazing intently at him with shining eyes.

"Forgive me!" said the bearded man in a weak voice, when he saw that the King was awake and was looking at him.

"I do not know you, and have nothing to forgive you for," said the King.

"You do not know me, but I know you. I am that enemy of yours who swore to revenge himself on you, because you executed his brother and seized his property. I knew you had gone alone to see the hermit, and I resolved to kill you on your way back. But the day passed and you did not return. So I came out from my ambush to find you, and I came upon your bodyguard and they recognized me and wounded me. I escaped from them, but should have bled to death had you not dressed my wounds. I wished to kill you, and you have saved my life. Now, if I live, and if you wish it, I will serve you as your most faithful slave and will bid my sons to do the same. Forgive me!"

The King was very glad to have made peace with his enemy so easily, and to have gained him for a friend, and he not only forgave him, but said he would send his servants and his own physician to attend him, and promised to restore his property.

Having taken leave of the wounded man, the King went out onto the porch and looked around for the hermit. Before going away he wished once more to beg an answer to the questions he had put. The hermit was outside, on his knees, sowing seeds in the beds that had been dug the day before.

The King approached him, and said: "For the last time, I pray you to answer my questions, wise man."

"You have already been answered!" said the hermit, still crouching on his thin legs, and looking up at the King, who stood before him.

"How answered? What do you mean?" asked the King.

"Do you not see," replied the hermit. "If you had not pitied my weakness yesterday and had not dug these beds for me, but had gone your way, that man would have attacked you and you would have repented of not having stayed with me. So the most important time was when you were digging the beds; and I was the most important man; and to do me good was your most important business. Afterwards, when that man ran to us, the most important time was when you were attending to him, for if you had not bound up his wounds he would have died without having made peace with you. So he was the most important man, and what you did for him was your most important business. Remember then: there is only one time that is important—*Now!* It is the most important time because it is the only time when we have any power. The most necessary man is he with whom you are, for no man knows whether he will ever have dealings with any one else: and the most important affair is, to do him good, because for that purpose alone was man sent into this life!"

Growing Old

One of the things they never warned me about growing old: The older you get, the greater the percentage of the people you know who are already dead. Continuing to meet young people helps a lot to slow down this process.

 —SA

I have heard that someone once asked Maurice Chevalier, "What is it like to be old?"

Chevalier replied: "Not bad, particularly when you consider the alternative."

—SA

It's good to be here.
At my age, it's good to be *anywhere.*

—George Burns at 100

An aged man is but a paltry thing,
A tattered coat upon a stick, unless
Soul clap its hands and sing, and louder sing
For every tatter in its mortal dress.

—W. B. Yeats

Reprinted with permission of Simon & Schuster, Inc. from THE POEMS OF
W.B. YEATS: A NEW EDITION, edited by Richard J. Finneran. Copyright 1928
by Macmillan Publishing Company, renewed 1956 by Georgie Yeats.

They are not long, the weeping and the laughter,
    Love and desire and hate:
I think they have no portion in us after
    We pass the gate.

They are not long, the days of wine and roses:
    Out of a misty dream
Our path emerges for a while, then closes
    Within a dream.

—Ernest Christopher Dowson

From "Vitae Summa Brevis," in *Anthology of World Poetry*, © 1936, Harcourt, Brace
& Co.

Wisdom

Old age doesn't guarantee wisdom,
But it does give you an opportunity.

—SA

When Pablo Casals reached 95, a young reporter threw him a question: "Mr. Casals, you are 95 and the greatest cellist that ever lived. Why do you still practice six hours a day?" Casals answered, "Because I think I'm making progress."

—BITS & PIECES, June 24, 1993

Death never takes the wise man by surprise;
He is always ready to go.

—Jean de la Fontane

Death

If you have ever been asked about death by a small child, you know how hard it is to give an honest and satisfactory answer. And without a good answer, the question will not go away, returning again and again, like the tides.

Stephen Jay Gould calls death "the most terrible datum." Other animals feel fear and pain, and flee danger, but as far as we know, no other creature foresees the inevitability of their own personal death. Most adults try to avoid this knowledge altogether, and it is probably no accident that every religion attempts to provide some kind of palatable answer to this terrible fact. Probably more has been written about death, and what might lie beyond it, than any other topic.

For me, personally, the evidence for an afterlife is not very compelling, and I live my life as if this is all there is. If we get to vote on reincarnation, I'll vote yes. I'd like to give life another try. But I suspect we don't get to vote.

—SA

It matters not how a man dies, but how he lives. The act of dying is not of importance, it lasts so short a time.

—Samuel Johnson

The Living Cemetery

I like to stroll among the stones
    where others fear to tread.
They say the stench of death is here
    and some have even said
That restless spirits lie in wait
    to swell the ranks of dead.

The touch they fear to feel at night
    when mist bleeds from the mold,
The icy finger beckoning
    beneath a mossy fold,
Would be, you see, a proof to me
    of what I'm often told.

A sign that death is not quite death
    but something more or less
Than complete annihilation
    and utter nothingness.
A sign that life, though changed, moves on
    though where, we might not guess.

I've walked these studded mounds at length.
    I've lain in grass that's grown
From dusty signatures of friends
    beside their fathers, sown.
The silence here is never rent
    by sound from under stone.

This silent voice denies each day
    the tales that prophets tell.
And all must bow and go their way
    when rings the dusty bell.
But no such death do I find here
    as where the living dwell.

The loss of love, the dying joy,
    is death enough to fear.
And he who dies this death must watch
    his spirit borne on bier.
He knows his pose of life is but
    a dry and cracked veneer.

No carven caskets lay to rest
    the life when love is spent.
No beauty stirs the stillborn joy
    beneath the shoulders bent
Upon the task of quarrying
    eternal monuments.

As death dies here, does life die there
    and likewise rots away
When life in quest of future blessed
    bends low its head to pray
For banal sin of permanence
    and loses bright today.

—SA (1960)

The Long Way

I am grateful for the haze
On the distance of my days.
If I saw too far ahead
I might turn about in dread
From the vastness of a plain
Measurable alone by pain.
And, beyond it, there in time
Mountains I might fear to climb.

One step forward—one step more—
Foot behind and foot before;
Standing safely, holding fast,
With a point of danger passed;
Drawing in the living breath,
Breathing out the fear of death,
Balanced so precariously
On impossibility.

—Robert Lee Brothers

From *Robert Lee Brothers: The Collected Poems* edited by Susan Ford Wiltshire, Ph.D. (in preparation).

Futility

Move him into the sun—
Gently its touch awoke him once,
At home, whispering of fields half-sown.
Always it woke him, even in France,
Until this morning and this snow.
If anything might rouse him now
The kind old sun will know.

Think how it wakes the seeds—
Woke once the clays of a cold star.
Are limbs, so dear achieved, are sides
Full-nerved, still warm, too hard to stir?
Was it for this the clay grew tall?
—O what made fatuous sunbeams toil
To break earth's sleep at all?

—Wilfred Owen (1918)

(Wilfred Owen was killed November 4, 1918, just seven days before the armistice ending World War I was signed.)

From Wilfred Owen: The Collected Poems of Wilfred Owen. Copyright © 1963 by Chatto & Windus Ltd. Reprinted by permission of New Direction Publishing Corp.

How Shall I Die?

How shall I die?
    Like a mouse
    held by yellow talons
    swiftly torn from life
    by the curved thrusting beak?
        Like a nest of water in sand and seaweed,
        scurrying creatures slowly gathered
        to a steaming stinking cluster
        by the ebbing tide?
            Or under a car, oozing red juice
            like a cherry crushed
            between the teeth of my own error
            in the shape of a slipping jack?

And what will my last sensation be?
    The tearing of my flesh,
    my body twisting in futile rebellion?
        A soft breeze stroking my belly
        cool respite from the heat and stench?
            A heavy throbbing ache
            intolerable pressure, briefly tolerated?

And who would change the moment of my death?
Rewrite the turning pages of the world
adjust page lengths, numbers, footnotes
to accomodate the new edition?
Snatch the mouse from the thrusting beak
to die belly up in the tide pool?
Steady the slipping jack
releasing me to another death
in another place?

No.
Death is a cruel gift
like life, it comes
unbidden, unsought, unscheduled.
A kind reminder to me
of what I have
as I live.

—SA (1975)

The Four Enemies of a Man of Knowledge

A man of knowledge is one who has followed truth-
fully the hardships of learning. A man who has, without
rushing or without faltering, gone as far as he can in un-
raveling the secrets of power and knowledge.

When a man starts to learn, he is never clear about his
objectives. His purpose is faulty; his intent is vague. He
hopes for rewards that will never materialize, for he
knows nothing of the hardships of learning. He slowly
begins to learn—bit by bit at first, then in big chunks.
And his thoughts soon clash. What he learns is never what
he pictured, or imagined, and so he begins to be afraid.
Learning is never what one expects. Every step of learning is a new task, and the fear the man is experiencing begins to mount mercilessly, unyieldingly. His purpose
becomes a battlefield.

And thus he has stumbled upon the first of his natural
enemies: Fear! A terrible enemy—treacherous, and difficult to overcome. It remains concealed at every turn of the
way, prowling, waiting. And if the man, terrified in its

presence, runs away, his enemy will have put an end to his quest. He will never become a man of knowledge. He will perhaps be a bully, or a harmless, scared man; at any rate, he will be a defeated man. His first enemy will have put an end to his cravings.

To overcome fear he must not run away. He must defy his fear, and in spite of it he must take the next step in learning, and the next, and the next. He must be fully afraid, and yet he must not stop. That is the rule! And a moment will come when his first enemy retreats. The man begins to feel sure of himself. His intent becomes stronger. Learning is no longer a terrifying task.

When this joyful moment comes, the man can say without hesitation that he has defeated his first natural enemy. It happens little by little, and yet the fear is vanquished suddenly and fast. Once a man has vanquished fear, he is free from it for the rest of his life because, instead of fear, he has acquired clarity—a clarity of mind which erases fear. By then a man knows his desires; he knows how to satisfy those desires. He can anticipate the new steps of learning, and a sharp clarity surrounds everything. The man feels that nothing is concealed.

And thus he has encountered his second enemy: Clarity! That clarity of mind, which is so hard to obtain, dispels fear, but also blinds. It forces the man never to doubt himself. It gives him the assurance he can do anything he pleases, for he sees clearly into everything. And he is courageous because he is clear, and he stops at nothing because he is clear. But all that is a mistake; it is like something incomplete. If the man yields to this make-believe power, he has succumbed to his second enemy and will be patient when he should rush. And he will fumble with learning until he winds up incapable of learning anything more. His second enemy has just stopped him cold from trying to become a man of knowledge; instead, the man may turn into a buoyant warrior, or a clown. Yet the clarity for which he has paid so dearly will never change to darkness and fear again. He will be clear as long as he lives, but he will no longer learn, or yearn for, anything.

To avoid being defeated he must do what he did with fear: he must defy his clarity and use it only to see, and wait patiently and measure carefully before taking new steps; he must think, above all, that his clarity is almost a mistake. And a moment will come when he will understand that his clarity was only a point before his eyes. And thus he will have overcome his second enemy, and will arrive at a position where nothing can harm him anymore. This will not be a mistake. It will not be only a point before his eyes. It will be true power.

He will know at this point that the power he has been pursuing for so long is finally his. He can do with it whatever he pleases. His ally is at his command. His wish is the rule. He sees all that is around him. But he has also come across his third enemy: Power!

Power is the strongest of all enemies. And naturally the easiest thing to do is to give in; after all, the man is truly invincible. He commands; he begins by taking calculated risks, and ends in making rules, because he is a master. A man at this stage hardly notices his third enemy closing in on him. And suddenly, without knowing, he will certainly have lost the battle. His enemy will have turned him into a cruel, capricious man. A man who is defeated by power dies without really knowing how to handle it. Power is only a burden upon his fate. Such a man has no command over himself and cannot tell when or how to use his power.

To defeat his third enemy, he has to defy it, deliberately. He has to come to realize the power he has seemingly conquered is in reality never his. He must keep himself in line at all times, handling carefully and faithfully all that he has learned. If he can see that clarity and power, without his control over himself, are worse than mistakes, he will reach a point where everything is held in check. He will know then when and how to use his power. And thus he will have defeated his third enemy.

The man will be, by then, at the end of his journey of learning, and almost without warning he will come upon the last of his enemies: Old age! This enemy is the cruelest of all, the one he won't be able to defeat completely, but only fight away.

This is the time when a man has no more fears, no more impatient clarity of mind—a time when all his power is in check, but also the time when he has an unyielding desire to rest. If he gives in totally to his tiredness, he will have lost his last round, and his enemy will cut him down into a feeble old creature. His desire to retreat will overrule all his clarity, his power, and his knowledge.

But if the man sloughs off his tiredness, and lives his fate through, he can then be called a man of knowledge, if only for the brief moment when he succeeds in fighting off his last, invincible enemy. That moment of clarity, power, and knowledge is enough.

—Carlos Casteneda

The Ex-Poet

Timber floats in the water. The trees
Arch over, it is green there, the shadow.
A child is walking on the meadow.
There is a sawmill, through the window.
I knew a poet once who came to this:
Love has not gone, only the words of love,
He said. The words have gone
Which would have painted that ship
Colors red lead never took
In sunsets livid at the Cape.
I said it was a good thing too.
He smiled and said: Someday
I shall have left this place as words left me.

—Malcolm Lowry

Leaves
Leaving everything
In green
In haste

To fall
Upon the past
Before my life can shudder
And begin its leap

Over time and understand
In Spring there
Are not many days
Or any

Left
To want—one perhaps,
Must have to leave
To love

      —From a poster by
    Sister Mary Corita Kent

Then

When the brook runs dry
and the dragonflies
come shimmering no more,
shadow-skipping over ripples,
and the frogs have departed
through browning ferns,
I shall arise and go,
stepping to the measure
of a slow forgetting
while memory follows
ever farther behind
in long drifts of fallen days.

—Robert Lee Brothers

From *Robert Lee Brothers: The Collected Poems* edited by Susan Ford Wiltshire, Ph.D. (in preparation).

The (Last) Rites Of Boko-Maru

God made mud.
God got lonesome.
So God said to some of the mud, "Sit up."
"See all I've made," said God, "The hills, the sea, the sky
    the stars."
And I was some of the mud that got to sit up and
    look around.
Lucky me, lucky mud.
I, mud, sat up and saw what a nice job God had done.
Nice going, God.
Nobody but you could have done it, God! I
    certainly couldn't have.
I feel very unimportant compared to You.
The only way I can feel the least bit important is to
    think of all the mud that didn't even get to sit up
    and look around.
I got so much, and most mud got so little.
Thank you for the honor!
Now mud lies down again and goes to sleep.
What memories for mud to have!
What interesting other kinds of sitting-up mud I met!
I loved everything I saw!
Good night. . . .

—Kurt Vonnegut Jr.

In Passing

In passing may the last thought in my mind
Be nothing shallow and yet not too deep
But something such as happy children find
In dreams that bring a smile into their sleep.

—Robert Lee Brothers

From *Robert Lee Brothers: The Collected Poems* edited by Susan Ford Wiltshire, Ph.D. (in preparation).

There are two wonderful stories that I couldn't get permission to reprint here. Luckily, they are both still in print, and available.

The Mountain that Loved a Bird, by Alice McLerran. Simon and Schuster.

Many Moons, by James Thurber and Louis Slobodkin. Harcourt, Brace, Jovanovich.

About The Author

Steve Andreas was born in Hawaii, and spent most of his growing up in the desert southwest: Arizona, Nevada, New Mexico, and California. A B.S. in chemistry from Caltech, and an M.S. in psychology from Brandeis University led to seven years of teaching psychology in a California Junior College. He started Real People Press in 1967, publishing books about alternative ways of understanding human living and potential. He was involved in Fritz Perls' Gestalt Therapy in the late 60's and 70's, and attempted to start a community based on Gestalt Therapy on an isolated ranch in Utah.

He now lives with his wife Connirae, and their three young sons (13, 11, and 9) in a small canyon valley in the foothills of the Rocky Mountains just north of Boulder, Colorado. For the last eighteen years Steve and Connirae have been deeply involved in Neuro-Linguistic Programming—a practical way of understanding how our brains and minds work that is useful both for working our way out of difficulties, and for moving toward discovering more about what it means to be a fully-functioning human being. They have edited four books about NLP, written three others, and have produced a number of NLP videotapes and audiotapes. They have also been active in developing a number of specific NLP patterns to help people heal emotionally and come to greater well-being and wholeness. They started NLP Comprehensive in 1979, which has developed into one of the foremost NLP training institutes in the U.S.

Index

211